YOU HAVE NO RIGHT TO STAY BROKEN

A Story-Guided Roadmap to Self-Actualization

TASHIYANNA NOEL

You Have No Right to Stay Broken: A Story-Guided Roadmap to Self-Actualization

Time to Get Over It Now is a division of (DBA) Mindwell Body + Soul, LLC
11800 N. Florida Ave. #17642
Tampa, FL 33612

ISBN 979-8-9866161-0-0 (hardcover)
ISBN 979-8-9866161-1-7 (paperback)
ISBN 979-8-9866161-2-4 (kindle edition)
Library of Congress Control Number: 2022913349
Printed in the United States of America.

The intent of this book is to offer education information to help you or a loved one over symptoms of anxiety and depression without the use of prescription drugs. The author does not dispense medical, psychological, spiritual, legal or financial advice or prescribe the use of any technique as a form of treatment without the advice of a professional. In the event you use the information within this book for yourself or a loved one, the author and publisher assumes no responsibility for your actions.

CONTENTS

This book is for all the courageous readers beginning their journey of self-discovery to self-actualization.

And my personal motivator, my son, Carter. You helped me find my purpose. You're the reason I aim to be better than I was the day before. I intend to give you the world, and that includes a healthy, happy mom.

APPLE OF MY EYE

It would've killed me to stay,

But it also pained me to leave.

Thinking of you without me,

When I knew you were all I'd need.

What almost brought me to my end,

Breathed life into the one I hated to love.

The one who broke me and embarrassed me,

Forever changing my life, I chose to rise above.

You made it worthwhile,

And I stole what I knew you needed most.

Everything I never had,

I'd hoped to give you all that and more.

But my love was just too much,

So I kept it safely stored.

Just for you I'd sacrifice,

Love of my life, sweetest apple of my eye.

In my heart you will remain,

You are my only sunshine.

INTRODUCTION

What makes a story personal? Is it the inherent nature of it being close to us – of having a solid account of the things and events we went through?

Or is it simply a string of words that we can somehow relate to?

Maybe it's a combination of all these that make a story relatable, giving the green light for us to consider it personal.

Like all stories, mine had a beginning. I don't mean there was emptiness before that. Although life seemed to become empty when both love and individuality were foreign to me.

But the conception of most stories have a foundation that can't be seen; like an iceberg, much of it is below the surface never to be accessed. Where our memories stay hidden, in a frozen state, tormenting our waking hours and stealing peaceful sleep.

We can't always identify what is happening to us as we're going through it. Is it general discomfort, fatigue, or a physical illness that fogs our brains? Or is it all in our minds to begin with?

We shrink ourselves, overpowered and defeated—not by others, but by our own selves trying to cope. Then one day we look in the mirror and fail to recognize ourselves due to how much has changed.

Our loved ones don't seem to understand. And no matter how much we try, an unmovable mountain seems to separate us from those we were once closest to. We lose motivation— and grow complacent living a life where we are undervalued and unappreciated.

But this is not how life is meant to be. Because isn't it true that every living thing holds some value?

And this is why we must do our best to preserve life, find our purpose, and be full of gratitude for what God has given us. We, as God's creation, are participants in an abundant circle of life. Our fulfillment lies in prevailing over sorrows and frustrations, and discovering peace and love.

Life is a journey of self-determination that is never easy. It's difficult to gather enough courage to stand before the mirror and say, "I am worthy of the best things in life just the way I am."

On the other hand, I know many like me suffer from incessant guilt, frustration, and depression. The thing is, unpleasant things that happen in our lives aren't always a failure or loss. Unfair incidents can even be seen as an opportunity that steers us to full development, opportunities we may have never come across had it not been for what we experienced.

I know this because I was just as traumatized as many of you are now. I too have suffered, desperate to let go of the hurt I was carrying, and it took me more than ten years of therapy, discontinuing psychotropic medications, and four years of intentional living to find a sliver of serenity and joy.

Today, I am a much more complete person for acknowledging my ego and faults. Finding my purpose gave me strength. I've stopped fighting daily wars with myself over small things. I am comfortable with who I am and what I truly believe in. Plus, my core values are now more refined and compatible with the life I desire to have.

Overall, my life is significantly more satisfying, and I wanted to share how I accomplished such satisfaction. Because I believe that when you share your abundance, your joy magnifies in various ways.

Together, we will set out on a journey to honor our own selves, making our lives more meaningful and harmonized, with a greater understanding and compassion for others and ourselves.

This book is not a substitute for professional help. Therapy works best when you are ready for change, when you like your therapist, and can commit to doing the work between sessions. However, if you still haven't found the right type of help or can't afford the help you feel you need at the moment, my hope is that through this book you rediscover your truth and become self-actualized so that you may live free of guilt or anger.

With Love,

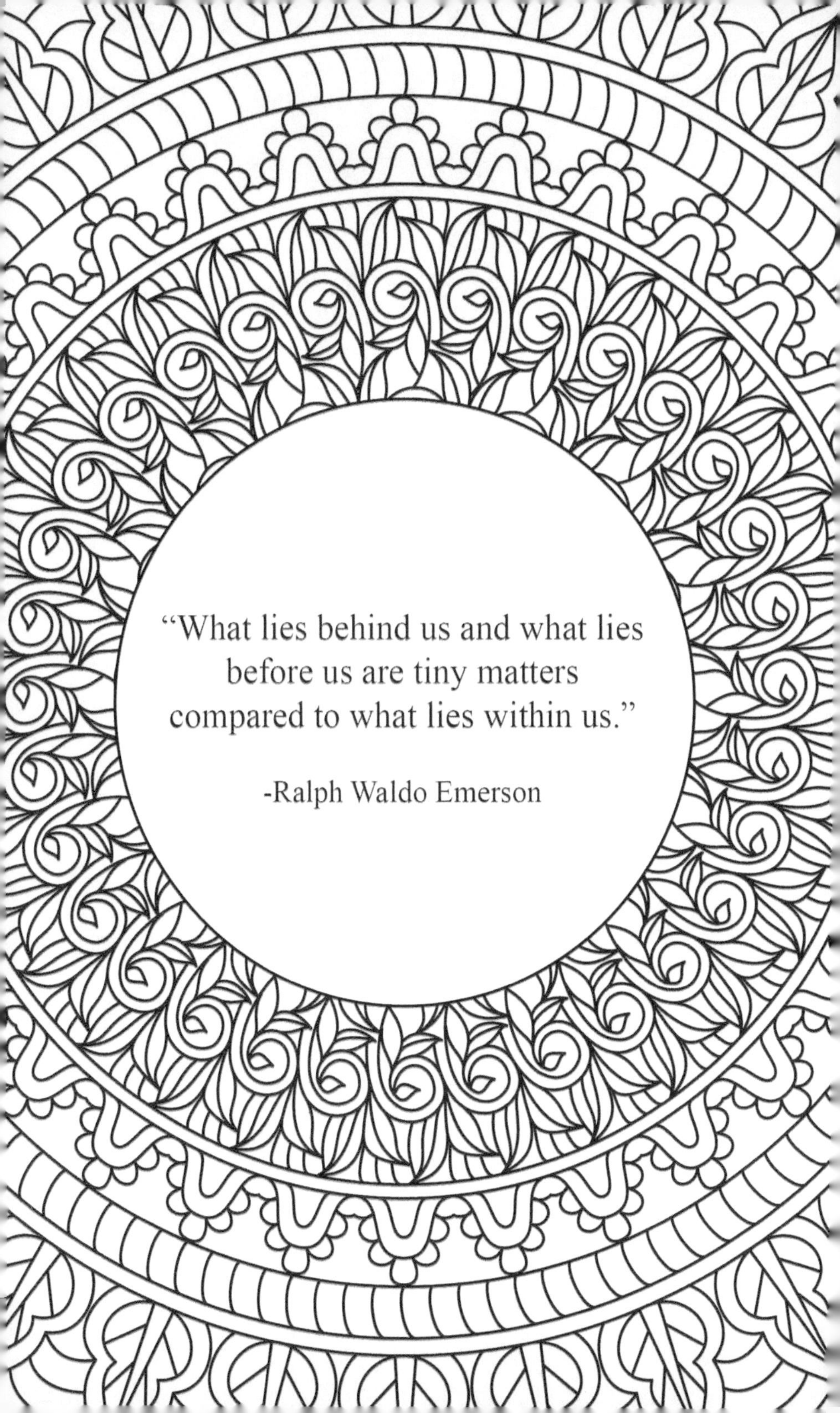
"What lies behind us and what lies
before us are tiny matters
compared to what lies within us."

-Ralph Waldo Emerson

Chapter One

THE PRELUDE

I HAVE BEEN PRESSURED to conform to other people's standards my whole life.

It started with critiques from my family, "Tash, don't sit with your back all hunched over like that."

Next, it was my peers who shamelessly judged me, "You don't shave your legs? You're disgusting!"

Then, my employers began to chastise me, "In order for you to succeed in life, you're going to have to learn to stop being emotional!"

And, let's not forget my dismissive ex-husband, "You're never going to make any friends if you don't start being nicer to people," he would say.

Their condescension, which is what it was even though I didn't see it at the time, was often intended as "constructive criticism", but any insight or explanation I provided for my actions was considered defensive or disrespectful. This was especially the case with the older people in my family, and later the men I worked for. So over time, I became more obliging.

I wanted to absorb the lessons of the people who thought themselves wiser. I strived to be a well-behaved child, an easy-going friend, a teachable employee, and a laidback partner. Welcoming their descriptions and opinions of me voluntarily, trying to make the people around me happy, slipping in and out of the different roles demanded of me.

Inside, I didn't agree with it all; a part of me grew sick at what I forced myself to do all the time to please others.

But I was young and didn't know better. Therefore, I figured if I could learn from the mistakes of others, I would be well on my way to being the smartest person in the room. But instead of learning something of value, I simply became sheeplike.

It took me years to realize how the things that were said to me, things that happened to me, or the things I'd witnessed had defined and molded me.

The same things I'd believed were rolling off my back had gravely affected me and, in fact, were shaping my everyday decisions and interactions.

Life for me was bittersweet, with so many ups and downs. It was hard to remain level-headed and consider future prospects while living on what felt like a rollercoaster ride. But from where I was standing, life wasn't fair for most people, so why waste time complaining?

I understood much later, while in therapy, that my problem was extreme reliability on other people's approval—again and again. I allowed myself to be swayed by tangled emotions, and in the act of "going with the flow" in the face of adversity I did nothing to stand up for myself, crushing my confidence and self-respect in the process.

FEELINGS WHEEL: TOOL FOR EMOTIONAL INTELLIGENCE

What helped me substantially wrap my head around what I was feeling about my past and open myself up to being vulnerable was first finding a therapist I could trust. Next, it was *The Feeling Wheel*.

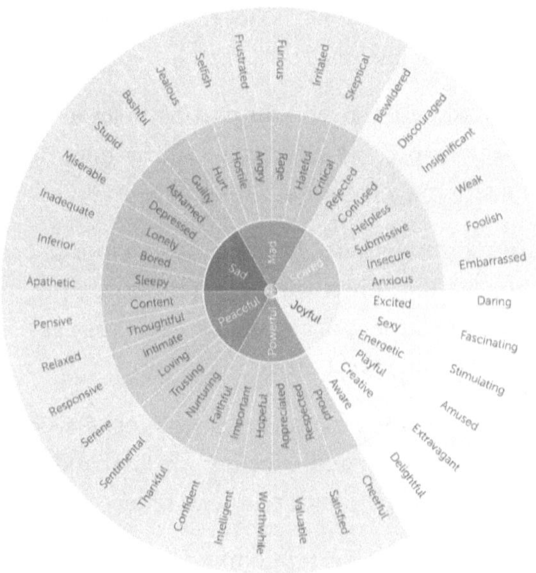

The Feeling Wheel
by Gloria Willcox

Designed first by Dr. Gloria Willcox, The Feeling Wheel starts in the center with the most general emotions we have been familiar with since childhood.

Then as you go beyond the center into the next ring, you will notice the feelings get a bit more complex, and the final outer ring provides even more insight into what it is you might be feeling.

This tool was designed to increase emotional intelligence and awareness, allowing you to identify, discuss, and ultimately control your emotions effectively.

STREAM OF CONSCIOUSNESS WRITING

In addition to therapy, journaling was a convenient, and practically free tool I used to improve my mental and emotional well-being–providing clarity when I was faced with difficult emotions or choices. Pen and paper were easily accessible and writing seemed to improve my communication skills. Plus, I never felt afraid of being judged after freely expressing my inner thoughts.

I didn't know it when I started, but writing in an unfiltered, stream of conscious way helped me clear some of my brain fog and better understand how to process my emotions.

Word of Caution: because I know how important it is to be vulnerable, honest, and open with yourself to get the most out of this transformative journey, if any of the exercises cause you to feel overwhelmed, stop and take a break.

Practice staying grounded by breathing in for 4 seconds, holding your breath for 7 seconds, and exhaling for 8 seconds. This specific breathing technique helps you to relax and reduce anxiety.

You can also use the 5-4-3-2-1 grounding technique. Start by looking around and naming five things you see. Next, determine four things you can feel. For instance, nod your head up and down, rotate your shoulders or ankles, or raise your eyebrows several times. Then focus on three distinct sounds you can hear, like a ticking clock, or outside noises, or you can even listen to the sound of your own breath as you use the 4-7-8 breathing technique. Next, focus on two things you can smell. Finally, make one affirming statement to yourself. For example, "I am strong and will continue taking small steps to overcome my limitations and accomplish my goals."

This helps you to get back into your body, stay in the present moment, and decreases your chances of slipping into a traumatic flashback or dissociation.

Exercise One: Processing Your Emotions

In your companion journal, or on a single sheet of paper, write down what you are feeling right now. What emotions are you trying to avoid, and what is preventing you from acknowledging these emotions?

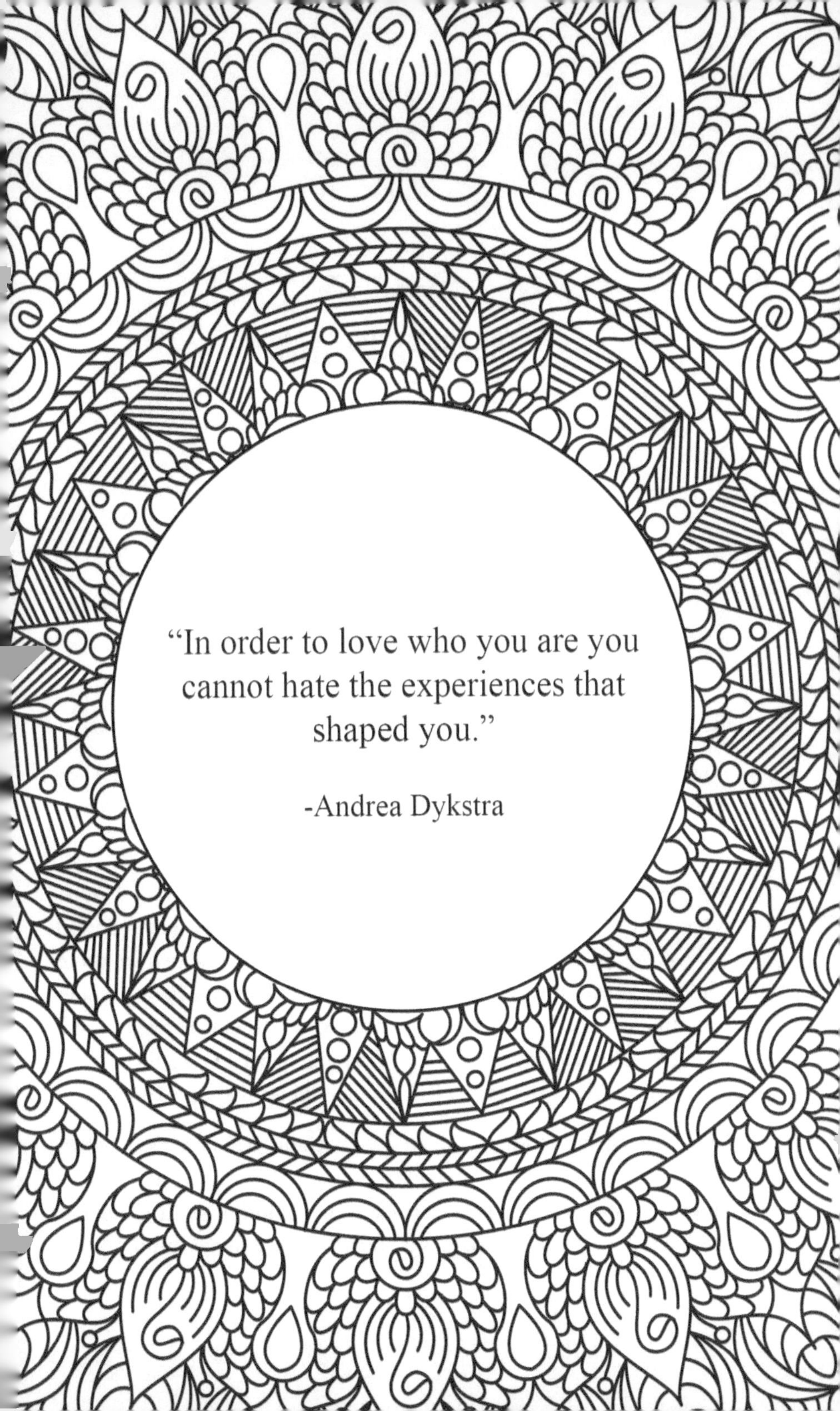

"In order to love who you are you cannot hate the experiences that shaped you."

-Andrea Dykstra

Chapter Two

THE FORMATIVE YEARS

LET'S begin at one of the most impactful events of my life—the first time I realized my life was not mine to control.

DETACHED SEPARATION

I was in middle school when my mother permanently moved my younger sister and me away from our hometown, Milwaukee, Wisconsin, to a suburb just outside of Denver, Colorado.

My parents had divorced when I was only three years old. I don't remember much of their relationship. But if the years that followed were any indicator of how things were between the two of them while they were together, I'm glad they parted ways. The anger and resentment they held for one another drove them, as well as my younger sister and me, mad. I can't imagine what life would've been like for us living in the same city, let alone under the same roof.

Nonetheless, my mother relocated us without our father's consent, hoping our standard of life would improve. She wanted us to avoid inner-city stereotypes, crime-stricken neighborhoods, and under-funded schools, and Colorado was the ideal place in her mind.

Maybe she worried about how my sister and I would adjust in a city where Blacks made up less than 1% of the total population. But even today, I'm not so sure. She was not the type of person to explain herself, especially to children. She always did what she thought was best, even if other people were involved.

And the state of Colorado wasn't completely unknown to us. My mother's father and elder brother lived there, and we'd visited them in the past. But it still took quite a bit of getting used to. We were completely oblivious, unfamiliar and uninformed when we arrived.

Like most single moms from impoverished backgrounds, my mother struggled in her desire to give her children more than she ever had. She made it known throughout our adolescent years that she expected us to make better choices than she did.

She had me, her firstborn, fresh out of high school. So, although she was very strict, she was young and full of life. She couldn't wait to send us back to our father each summer and enjoy her free time. It was something she looked forward to every year.

However, while in her care throughout the year we had as much fun as possible. We would play outside, go to the mall or to the movies often. But because my mother used one of her friend's addresses when registering us for school, it was unusual for us to get together with kids we went to school with.

Additionally, my mother was a preacher of *what happens in our house, stays in our house*. Meaning other kids rarely stayed over, regardless of how well she knew their parents.

As a result, my closest "friends" were the children I met over the summer in Milwaukee, rather than the people I spent most of my time with throughout the year.

But for me, Milwaukee had been a life before Denver. By this point I'd spent over a decade in the inner-city, and the difference between where we came from and where we wound up was dramatically different. In Milwaukee we might have been "underprivileged" but I had food for sustenance, safe drinking water, shelter for security, and felt as if I belonged. In Colorado, however, there may have been more advantages but I definitely didn't feel as if I belonged.

I initially saw Colorado as the root cause of my misery. Outside of school and the occasional visit to church with my uncle, there was minimal interaction with people outside of our immediate family. I found it quite difficult to build genuine friendships with kids from school because we had nothing in common. So I spent a lot of my time in the house on my phone or on the internet, similar to most children today.

I'm not sure why I was so desperate for a social life. I was still a child, after all. And you're probably thinking, *a young child shouldn't need to do a lot of things*. And I agree. Maybe it was it a sign I was ahead of my time. I'm not quite sure. But, I never had the full privilege of enjoying my childhood.

And as I developed, technically, there were more things to do. But, I put majority of my energy into accomplishing what was expected of me, with the intention of staying off punishment so I could do the things I enjoyed.

Eventually I got involved in extracurricular activities. I was naturally skilled in volleyball so it quickly became my favorite. And by 14 I was gainfully employed. I made pretzels at a place in the mall, and even modeled a bit. I also spent a lot of time researching schools trying to determine where I wanted to go to college.

My parents laid out what was expected of me, and the list seemed to grow longer every year. Although I found myself in trouble every now and then for things like talking in class, I was an excellent student. I maintained all As and Bs in my classes, including several advanced courses I was taking for college credit. I even helped pay bills sometimes. I did everything that was asked of me even when I didn't understand it.

I did not realize then that my behavior, while bringing academic success and appreciation from my family, would create a huge imbalance in my personal life as I became an adult.

Exercise Two: Addressing Your Inner Child

Envision yourself at whatever age when you felt that you needed the most support. What do you look like? What are you doing? In your companion journal, or on a separate sheet of paper, write down five things that you would say to your childhood self that would make "little you" smile.

ENDURING TRAUMA AS A YOUNG ADULT

I was still in high school when I tried to take my own life for the first time. I'd grown resentful and weary and took a handful of Excedrin, ready to give up on life.

When my mother discovered me, she made me vomit and put me under a cold shower.

She then told me how she'd been in my shoes. She called my attempts to give up on life a "stunt", that would only result in me getting my stomach washed out with charcoal. I assumed this was her way to deter me from making any more attempts. Unfortunately, that wouldn't be the case.

I eventually started seeing my school guidance counselor. She encouraged me to contact my father and tell him what was going on. In her opinion, I wasn't a suicidal person; I was instead running from my problems. And on some level, I knew my counselor was right, but I didn't know what else I could do to rid myself of the sadness I felt all the time.

I was young and naïve; the reasons for my bouts of anxiety and depression were unclear to me at the moment. My emotions were too knotted for me to untangle and describe what I was feeling to another person. I just knew I didn't want to continue on the way I had been.

I'd had my virginity stolen by someone who lived with us, and after finally working up the courage to share this with my mother and step-father, believe it or not, they placed the blame squarely on my undeveloped shoulders.

To add insult to injury, they asked me for proof, and when I could only show them a stained comforter, they advised me to stop walking around the house in my volleyball shorts and lock my door at night.

It turned out my mother had labeled me a pathological liar. She thought I'd made up the whole thing to get my way and instead of taking the time to discover the facts life continued as usual for her. So, what could I do but mimic her attitude? I did my best to pretend it never happened hoping to avoid upsetting her further.

But, in the process, I got the message that it was more important to maintain an image of an unaffected and well-brought-up girl, even though that meant ignoring my concerns of feeling unsafe in my own home.

It's possible she spoke to my abuser in private because he never touched me again after that night, but something in me changed forever.

There was clearly a lack of trust and understanding between my mother and me. I worried about what would happen if my father found out, or other family members, and if I should involve the police. I was afraid not just for myself but also for my little sister. Outwardly though, I maintained my composure—or at least I thought I did.

Every day, I got up and went to school as I normally would. I did my chores, went to work, and counted down the days until I would be free and independent from my mother's tyranny—even after my abuser moved out, about a year later.

Meanwhile, I began to look elsewhere for support and love, and bent over backward to satisfy new expectations of who, and how, I should be.

The same girls who'd bullied me for not shaving my legs (along with things like using pads instead of tampons, and for not wearing makeup) encouraged me to visit chat rooms and websites that my parents told me to avoid. But, in order to belong I felt I had to do what they were doing. I needed to apply just the right amount of makeup to be considered "beautiful"—not too much and not too little. I couldn't just shave my armpits, I had to shave my legs and arms too. It was about following and achieving their standard, not my own.

The boys were no less difficult to navigate. I'd been taught by my father that boys only wanted one thing. Afraid to share myself with anyone, I ignored most of their advances. Instead, I tried relating to them through camaraderie, participating in their pranks, and allowing them to cheat off my tests.

I was the ultimate people pleaser. I had a hard time saying 'no' to anyone. I grew dependent on the love and affection of others, portraying myself as a helpful, dependable, beautiful person, versus the miserable and angry person I felt inside.

I was lending myself to help relieve the burdens others' were carrying, hardly noticing how my shoulders were chaffed from over-use. Hopelessly trying to cope with adversity, feeling like I was dying on the inside.

Despite my attempts to conform to life in Colorado, I felt different, like my teenage years were not those of a typical teenager. Later in life, when I reflected on these years, I began to understand what adolescence is really all about. It is the beginning of puberty, and it starts from an average of 9.5 to 14 years old, indicating hormonal changes in our bodies that affect not just our thinking but our mental processes too.

In comparison to puberty, childhood is a relatively carefree period of our lives. Everything is being taken care of, including each and every minor discomfort. A child instinctively knows how to maneuver around and manipulate their caregivers, when to obey orders and when to throw tantrums. Even if they are a bit disobedient, their mothers would not love them any less.

However, it is harder for girls than it is for boys. Girls have to make more adjustments and fit into the norms. Although society and technology have made a lot of progress, technological advancements have simultaneously made it difficult in other ways. For example, adolescents are more exposed to social media and social media culture, vulnerable to losing connections with the real world and building genuine relationships.

Parents, especially mothers, are more strict with girls; therefore, their exposure to society remains much more restricted than exposure for boys, leaving young females more vulnerable to outside influences.

As we look into what these puberty changes mean, we will better understand how these very special periods of our lives will affect us later as we become adults.

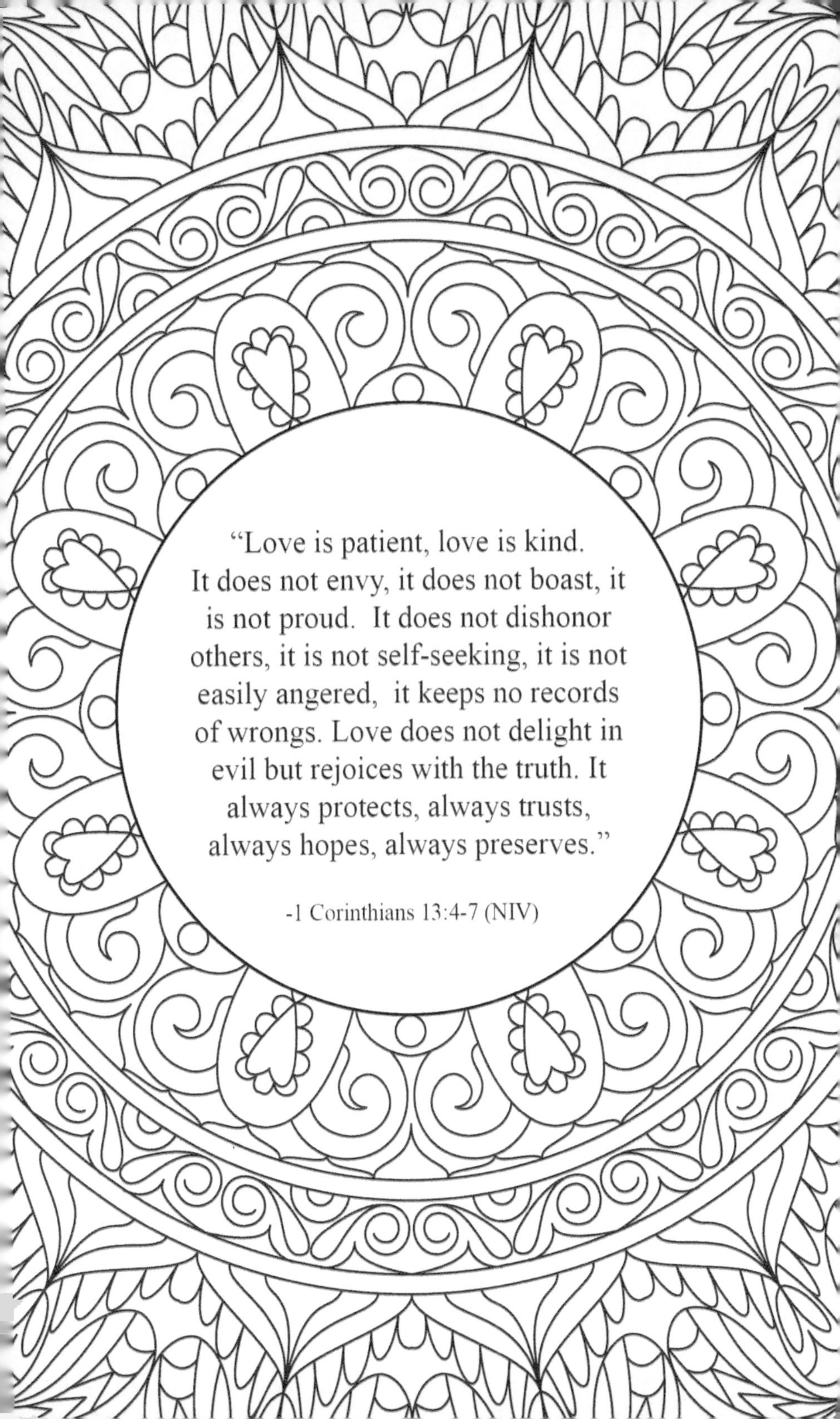

"Love is patient, love is kind.
It does not envy, it does not boast, it
is not proud. It does not dishonor
others, it is not self-seeking, it is not
easily angered, it keeps no records
of wrongs. Love does not delight in
evil but rejoices with the truth. It
always protects, always trusts,
always hopes, always preserves."

-1 Corinthians 13:4-7 (NIV)

THE ERRATICISM OF YOUNG ADULTHOOD

OUR TEENAGE YEARS are a period of rapid transformations. Cognitive neuroscientist and expert on the teenage brain, Sarah-Jaynes Blakemore, explains that the challenges a teenager faces are considerably unique – describing it as the "perfect storm" due to the large amount of emotional, hormonal, neurological, and social changes that take place during this phase of life.

When on the brink of adulthood but not quite considered by grownups as functional members of society, these changes are harder to grasp mentally and emotionally. Our undeveloped bodies undergo growth spurts and puberty changes, which can be difficult to process using our immature teenage brains. Furthermore, we've yet to learn the "ways of the world in a social context."

The most helpful thing is stable support and empathy from our parents during this time. Unfortunately, my mother didn't support me or provide understanding when I approached her about the abuse I'd suffered. Things surely would have turned out much differently for me if this had been the case!

This type of care shapes our personality, forcing our temperament to adapt in an inconsistent way. It evolves our thinking, behavior, and emotions. Though I can't entirely blame my mother–though she should have looked into my allegations–due to the individualistic nature of teenagers during this period of time, the parent-child relationship is naturally disturbed. Blame it on the hormonal changes and the lack of ability to think and reason during this period of time.

I'm sure you remember the messy rooms and mood swings from your teenage years. There are scientific reasons behind this.

A Dutch study involving thousands of teenagers that began in 2005 and lasted for seven years, showed that adolescent girls showed a temporary rise in neuroticism and the boys developed a temporary lack of discipline and carefulness. Dr. Blakemore and other researchers reported that if there is any adversity as a result of the teenager's own actions, the situation creates more stress for them.

Therefore, parents should support their teenagers and love them harder and more openly. Because of my mother's seeming indifference, I suffered conflict. *Was I to blame for my abuse? Was it my fault?* Instead of placing the blame on our "guest", my caregivers blamed me for wearing clothing that invited sexual abuse. In my own home, the place where I should have felt the safest and the most accepted, I was made to feel ashamed and to blame for what happened. This followed me into adulthood.

Young adulthood, in my opinion, is the most important defining period of human life. A teenager is not yet out of the sheltered embrace of childhood, but so much is expected of them. Yet parents and teachers hardly prepare teenagers for such prominent changes. If anything, they seem to be watchful of what's coming *their* way–rebellion against the rules and structure they've meticulously established–without trying to ready their children for the life ahead.

Mothers obsess over their daughters, telling them repeatedly not to make the same stupid mistakes they did and fathers want their sons to make them proud. The teens, on the other hand, just want to live their lives as carefree and fun-filled as possible. After all, a teenager can enjoy such a special and exciting rite of passage only once.

These years are about maturing: not just physically, but also mentally. It is a time for intense feelings, falling in love, facing anguish and agonies, dealing with self-esteem issues, and mounting pressures. But besides this, teens exhibit other behaviors like sleeping more, becoming very moody and crabby without any apparent reason, and being highly conscious about body image.

This is because their bodies are changing rapidly, sometimes overnight. Males grow taller and lankier, with an increase in body and facial hair; their voices change—from innocent, little boy sweetness to a deeper, more masculine timbre. But it's not an easy change from boy to man, as their long, growing limbs make them clumsy, their voices crack from high to low and their genitals start reacting in unexpected, uncontrollable ways—often at the most embarrassing times.

Similarly, this transition is just as difficult for girls if not more. Girls often mature physically and mentally earlier than boys, sometimes as early as nine or ten years old. The shapes of their bodies change with the emergence of breasts, widened hips and a curved waistline. Plus, their monthly cycles begin—while this is sometimes celebrated as "a girl becoming a woman", often girls find themselves bewildered and disgusted by this inconvenient, sometimes unexpected, event.

Of course, both boys and girls become curious about these changes, but might be uncomfortable with asking adults about them because they're at an age when adults seem to be lacking insight and knowledge. Instead, teens feel that no one else can possibly understand them. So they turn to their peers for acceptance as well as information. During this is also when we become more conscious of social issues and politics as individuals.

This is why I turned to the very girls who bullied me for not being just like them—the ones who made fun of me throughout the school year for being immature and naive. They seemed to have the worldly knowledge I didn't possess.

Little did I know, all teenagers wrestle with advice on what to do, where to go, how to behave, and how to dress. I had no idea that my peers were being educated on societal norms, relationships, and career paths. What I didn't realize is that every teen feels like the whole world is criticizing them; like they can't hide from the daggers, dirty looks, and pressure. And having these feeling exploited can lead to problems such as sexual promiscuity, depression, and giving in to peer pressure even when it's contrary to the way they were raised by their family and their core beliefs.

Children will love their parents and look up to them. But, they are also eager to carve out their own paths as young adults. And, trust me, they are counting down the days until they can strike out on their own and find freedom!

HOW OUR YOUNGER YEARS SHAPE US

Teenagers can tell their parents what they want and need. After all, only the person wearing the shoe can tell you exactly where the shoe pinches. My teenage years however, were in turmoil, so I didn't feel as comfortable expressing myself. And when I did, I was often not heard because my mother and father were absorbed elsewhere. I felt abandoned and insignificant, consequently developing unhealthy defense mechanisms and coping skills to survive.

To feel insignificant to your parents is a different kind of rejection. Instead of being valued by the people you value the most—and expect the most from—their attitude towards you isolates and hardens you, and you feel as if something inside of you has died. And although your circumstances may not have been as unstable as mine, it's possible for you to have been traumatized by your own experiences.

Issues like class, gender, and racial inequities are clear to children. Although learned from a naive perspective, they influence their development. The idea of a person having a "core belief" originated from Cognitive Behavioral Therapy, which Professor Aaron Beck created in the 1960s.

According to Beck, we are given a set of beliefs in the earliest stages of child development and continue to redefine them through various experiences and interactions with others. What this means is that those closest to us, particularly our parents, are the primary people who influence the formation of our core beliefs and values.

Aristotle famously said, "Give me a child until they are seven, and I will show you the man or woman." At seven years old, we still believe our parents are the strongest people on earth. They're supreme beings in our eyes, and we hang on to their every word. I know I did, with mine. However, the thoughts that support our values and beliefs don't begin to affect us until much later, when we start making decisions for ourselves.

Sadly, the time of my life when I most could have benefitted from the wisdom my mother had accumulated, was the time I was least likely to ask for it—and for some reason, she was unable to willingly give it. Instead, I was made to feel worthless and unloveable.

Beck's cognitive theory further explains how people who harbor critical, or negative, core beliefs are more prone to depression in adult life. Likely because when this happens to us, especially when we're children, we have a hard time shaking these beliefs as adults. More than any other core values we may have learned, these negative thought patterns continue to affect us.

This type of negative core belief system makes us our inner voices very critical and is harmful as it causes us to diminish ourselves in our day-to-day living. We say things to ourselves like:

- *I'm not good enough.*
- *I'm a failure.*
- *The world is not safe.*

- *I can't do anything right.*
- *People can't be trusted.*
- *No one cares, so why try?*

What we feed ourselves daily shapes our thoughts, feelings, actions and behaviors. When we think about failure, even before we have ventured on a task, can essentially hold us back. This negative self-talk, or constantly reliving traumatic and painful memories from the past, reinforces beliefs associated with personal vulnerability and inferiority, fear that we are incapable of obtaining love and affection, or believing ourselves to be a burden to others. Our negative core values keep us believing that happiness is something just outside our reach.

Here's a more conventional example less rooted in trauma. When I was in high school, even before I started modeling, I wanted to be a singer. When my mother found out I was serious, she was more excited about it than I was. She bought me all kinds of music, and encouraged me to join the choir. She even let me apply for American Idol and took me to a casting.

But I was afraid of failing her. I thought I wasn't good enough and I would be wasting everyone's time. I didn't even attempt to complete tryouts. The moment I found out there were several rounds of auditions I asked to go home. My negative core beliefs preemptively prevented me from trying.

Later on, I regretted not trying for what I wanted. I wanted to try again years later, but never did. When fear of failure or other limiting beliefs stop you from going after something you truly want, you often fail to realize your full potential, and you're often not even aware of this deep-rooted issue.

You remain unsteady and nervous throughout your life, believing you are incompetent with few skills or talent. Your belief systems sabotage you, making you insecure, even if you are surrounded by supportive friends or family, and have enough money in your bank to experience financial freedom.

Like the ocean, which can't quench the thirst of someone adrift despite holding an enormous quantity of water, you remain full of unrealized potential.

Consider if your boss were to give you a raise, and say, "Your work is very good, and the company likes what you do, but we'd like you to increase your client interaction," (or whatever relates to your work). If you have a critical inner voice, you will focus solely on the last part of that statement and ignore the raise and "good work" part of it. Because of your limiting beliefs, you can't acknowledge what is good.

You instinctively cling to only the second, more negative part of their feedback because it suits what you believe about yourself. In this instance you are decidedly unhappy and most likely will blame yourself for not being even better, and then will act resentful towards your boss which will certainly not help your position at work, creating a vicious blame game cycle.

Exercise Three: Identifying Your Inner Wounds

In your companion journal, or on a separate sheet of paper, answer the following journal prompt. How did you perceive yourself during your childhood? Describe your attitudes and feelings toward your family/parents as a teenager.

Tap into your inner child and teenage self and imagine what they would say. If things weren't so great, write about the reasons why.

COMING TO TERMS WITH YOUR PAST

When I look back upon my teenage days, I remember spending a lot of time by myself. I would imagine a man who would someday save me from my pathetic excuse for a life.

I felt helpless and undesired. Plus, I had no real social life, so as an alternative I spent a lot of time talking to friends and family back home in Wisconsin. Then dial up internet blew up, and when we were given access to a computer at home, I became addicted.

The internet became a way to escape my bored, and going online every day became a matter of course. If I could log in, I made sure to do just that—break free!

By freshman year, it was customary for me to chat with different people on AIM, or social media sites like Myspace or BlackPlanet, sometimes even under a fake name. My online friends, of whom there were many compared to my friends in real life, stayed virtual. It did not matter where they lived, if their identities were real, or if I was being catfished. They were a distraction, a form of entertainment, and just something for me to do.

As a teenager whose formative years were spent seeking validation from others, my advice to teenagers, and adults alike, with a difficult past would be to accept your past as part of your journey. Find the lesson in the pain and focus on the good; use it to discover how you can help others like you who may have experienced something similar. We are all born with natural abilities, but sometimes they need to be pulled out of us and sharpened in order for us to see and appreciate them. With enough positive reinforcements, you can absolutely mold your strengths into an inspirational success story.

Love and support from friends and family, specifically during those teenage years, is the type of positive reinforcements that help us to face life everyday stressors more easily. Parents provide security, safety, and a sense of belonging for their children. While true friends help us acknowledge our strengths without criticizing our weaknesses. In a perfect scenario an adolescent will learn self-responsibility, but what's most important is self-confidence. It's critical to learn to acknowledge our natural capabilities as an integral part of our personalities, and view our weaknesses as areas to work on in order to survive and live well.

This mindset typically fosters self-compassion without rousing the harsh inner critic that says, "you're worthless," "you're a loser," or "no one wants you." However, in the event that you're one of many who didn't grow up with a perfect childhood, you will need to unlearn inherited toxic traits and coping mechanisms that no longer serve you, and work to change your negative core beliefs the same way I had to.

HOW TO CHANGE NEGATIVE CORE BELIEFS

Let's take a moment to talk about what's known as "cognitive reframing". This means to consider your belief system and challenge its validity in real-life situations. What this does is reveals our "cognitive distortions," those ideas we assume to be accurate but are actually rooted in self-doubt and fear. For me, criticisms my mother had told me, like "You overreact to everything", were instilled.

It took me recognizing that the belief that I tended to overreact to things had become a part of my usual thought process, which then enabled me to change my thoughts from negative to positive. I went from believing I was dramatic and overly emotional, to understanding that my mother just didn't have the capacity to put up with my reactions no matter what they were, and instead of saying as much she criticized me.

That's when I began to feel and act more confident. My mother's statement about me overreacting to things had everything to do with her—and nothing to do with me. Of course, I may have been emotional sometimes, but I was also a teenager. Being emotional is what teenagers—with a combination of hormones, immaturity and confusion—do. It's normal. I was normal, and so were my reactions. So, later when my partner would call me a hypochondriac, although I was triggered, I was able to dismiss his accusations and seek out the help I needed.

Learning to challenge my thought processes and analyze them against real-life situations wasn't easy at first. But by questioning my inner critic and asking, *"Do you really not have anyone in your corner?"* or *"Are you really not good at* anything, *or are you just not good at this?"* taught me the valuable skill of cognitive reframing.

Similarly, we can question our belief system about the world and its people. Negative core beliefs are damaging to our personal health, but those negative perspectives about others or the world also promote feelings of hopefulness. Here are some tips for you to learn this skill too:

Triggers

Analyze your thought patterns and ask yourself whether you consistently struggle with critical self-talk in a particular situation or around a specific person. Anything or anyone can trigger you; even a scent. It's up to you to not be triggered and to lead your mind away from those negative thought patterns but until you recognize them, you will struggle with changing them.

Origin

After you've determined your triggers, ask yourself: "Why do I think like this?"

All your thoughts come from someplace in your past. When you were a child, you didn't automatically assume the worst about yourself. As children we didn't think anything about our behavior at all, we just acted. It was the adults around us who passed judgment.

What judgments did you hear? Were they true—or were they just critical statements those adults might have heard when they were children, and then passed on to you? What statements triggered your negative beliefs about yourself? What are the reasons behind you feeling anxious or insecure?

Dare Yourself

You should remember this if you want to rescue yourself from depression: Your thoughts are not facts. If you want to get better, you have to get rid of your excuses. Which means you should challenge your negative thoughts and inner critic; when you do this, you will find out for yourself what happens when you face your fears and do the impossible. If you fail, and you might, at least you will be able to say that you tried, which is much better than having regrets.

- But first, prepare yourself for whatever it is; it can be an event, a presentation, a drastic change, or even choosing to travel abroad alone. Make an informed decision with the advice of others being taken into consideration, but follow your instincts. The outcome of your effort will be yours. However, keep in mind, there are no negative outcomes, because even if you don't accomplish exactly what you wanted there will still be something of value you can take from the experience.

- Listen carefully to others, and communicate openly but empathically. Appreciate differences.

- Believe in yourself; loving yourself teaches others how to value you.

Exercise Four: Appreciating Where You've Come From

In your companion journal, or on a separate sheet of paper, write down important life events that helped you shape your life and why these memories stuck out most. Pick one, or many, and write about how different the event may have played out if you were in a different place mentally and/or emotionally.

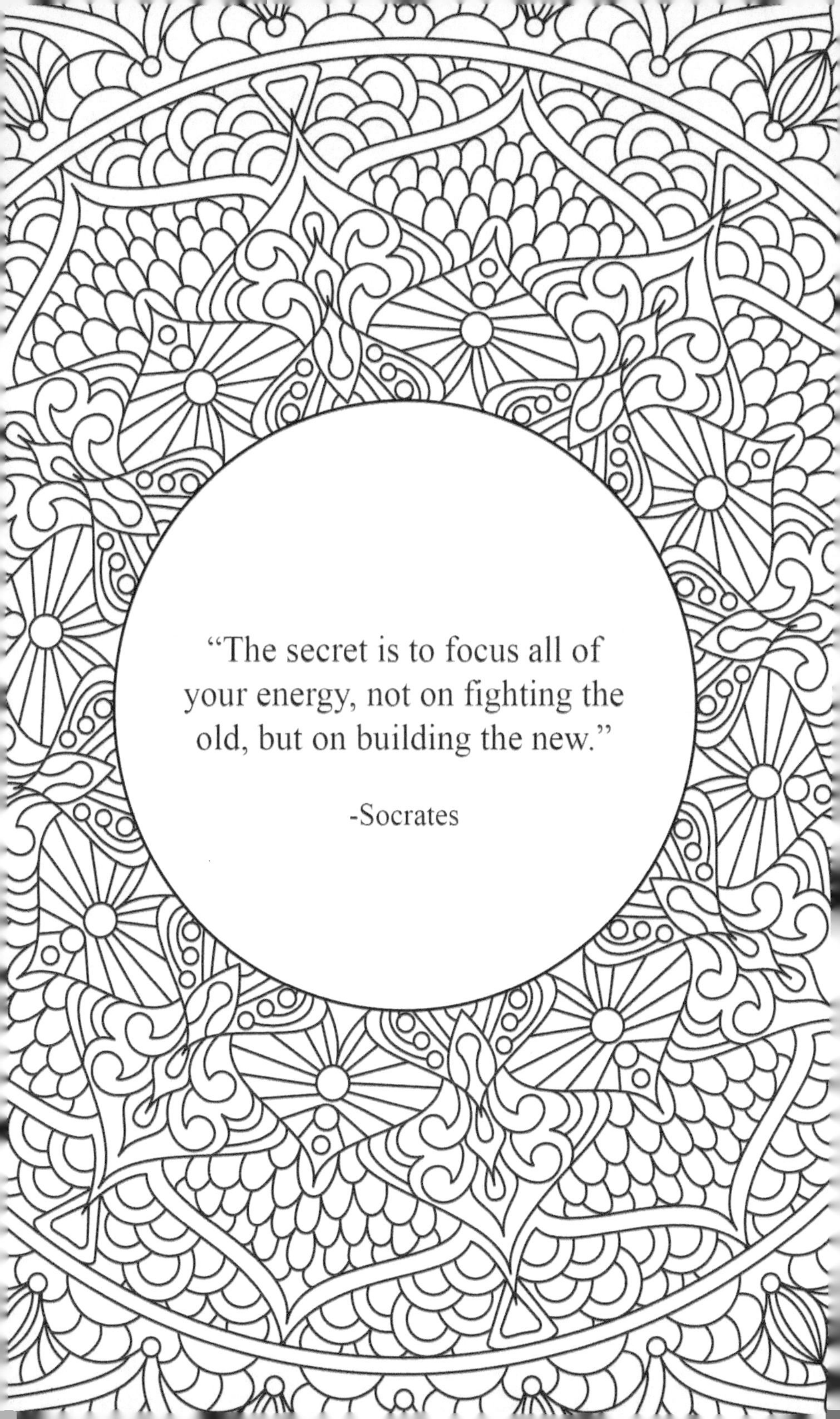

"The secret is to focus all of your energy, not on fighting the old, but on building the new."

-Socrates

Chapter Four

WHAT IS LOVE?

FALLING FOR A STRANGER

THE FIRST DAY I connected with my now ex-husband, I just so happened to be using my real profile on Myspace. I was a senior in high school, and although I can't recall the very first conversation we had, or who reached out to whom, I vividly remember what I loved about our virtual courtship.

We would post surveys, or questionnaires, on bulletin boards in groups we were both a part of with sometimes subtle, and sometimes not so subtle, subliminal messages for one another. We posted at least once every day, as our way of letting the other know we were thinking of them.

I was absolutely smitten with this online stranger who said and did all the right things. Towards the end of my senior year, we'd made it a priority to get to know each other better. We exchanged numbers and began texting. We shared pictures, and talked whenever we weren't working. By this time, I was graduating. I was seventeen and independent, headed off to college, and was happy to pay any overage charges at the end of the month if it meant keeping our line of communication open.

We had plenty in common so there was always something to talk about—we were both creative writers, him an aspiring musician and me, an aspiring author. We'd both modeled, and we shared the same zodiac sign. Although he was older than me by four years, not once did I believe he wasn't who he made himself out to be. I quickly fell head over heels in love and we had yet to even meet him in real life.

Then, after dating long-distance for almost a year he broke up with me to date someone else his parents felt was better suited for him. He said our relationship was too difficult to navigate considering his needs were going unmet. Not to mention, he felt being with me was draining because I had lost my grandmother a few years prior and was still grieving the loss years later.

He insisted that death was a natural part of life, and because a few years had passed, there was no reason to still be emotional about it.

At the time I didn't know how to articulate what was going on with me. I was finally alone for the first time at college, constantly worrying about my mom and sister. I couldn't get him to understand how losing our family's matriarch had continued to take a tremendous toll on my entire family, specifically my mother. Without my grandmother, our once tight-knit family had grown apart. Aunts, cousins, even siblings no longer communicated.

Nevertheless, he'd convinced me that I was grieving wrong. I don't know if it was the love I had for him, or just plain ignorance, but I agreed to better manage my emotions by reflecting on happier times so as to not be a burden. But at the end of the day, it wasn't enough. We decided to end things and hoped to remain friends.

A NAÏVE LOVE STORY

And remain friends we did, even while dating other people. When his new relationship ended several months later, he told me he wanted to get back together. He confessed he had never been in a monogamous relationship before. He claimed most women didn't possess enough of the characteristics he desired, therefore, he had always felt the need to date multiple women. Me, on the other hand, I was the only woman he'd met that made him want to be with just one person.

At the time I was single, so I was thrilled to hear him professing his love for me. I'd previously broken up with the guy I was seeing after I caught him cheating, and promptly cut him off. So, there was nothing to prevent me from saying agreeing to get back together.

Not for a second did I stop to think about how poorly he'd made me feel when we broke up. How he hadn't supported me in my time of grief, but I'd always been a shoulder for him to lean on in his times of need. Nor did I think about what his confession might say about the type of person he was. Instead, I felt accepted and validated because after the break I'd began to feel hopeless once again. So, without hesitation, I said yes to and we picked things back up right where we'd left them.

He flew to Colorado to see me, not too long afterwards and of course, I invited him to stay at my place. He'd been a friend and confidant, and I felt that I could trust him. I had my own apartment, and we were both eager to finally spend some quality time together in real life. Although it felt like we'd known each other our whole lives, we both knew there was still so much to learn about one another.

And as the days passed, naturally our level of intimacy evolved from emotional to physical. There was lots of kissing and touching at first. But when it came time for us to take things to the next level, his body was unresponsive.

Every attempt we made to be physically intimate that weekend was unsuccessful, and I was more than just disappointed, I felt embarrassed—but not even for him. I honestly blamed myself, and my insecurities never really let up.

He reassured me his lack of performance had nothing to do with me, and the issue was likely due to the vow he'd made with God to remain abstinent during his trip. It was an explanation I couldn't refute without sounding selfish. So, I convinced myself he was being straight with me, and moved on. In hindsight, of course, it was a huge red flag, but at the time I ignored it.

After he returned home, we continued our long-distance relationship. For a brief period of time things were great. But, after a few months he began to complain about the distance again. Then, later when I went to visit him at his family's home in Georgia over the summer, he proposed.

There was no confession of love, or anything special for that matter, although I do recall being shocked when I found the small box. Then he said, "I know you're going to say *yes*, so there's no need for me to get down on one knee," and slid the ring on my finger. I don't even remember my response.

I was a teenager trying to be an adult, with no real life examples to follow. I remember thinking, *Is this romantic?* It wasn't ideal because it was far from what I'd imagined for myself. But I told myself he loved me and was honest, and that was what truly mattered.

Besides, I thought, I was just being emotional, expecting a fairy tale, just like he'd accused me of in the past. And just like everyone else said I was. I needed to get over my romantic dreams and forget about grand gestures and scenes from movies. This was the real world and no one had that kind of romance in the real world. So, instead of listening to my own gut, I said *yes* and returned to Colorado as a fiancée.

Soon after, how we'd solve the issue of distance became a recurring topic of conversation. He said if we were going to be together, I needed to relocate. His move to Atlanta hadn't panned out the way he'd hoped, so he was moving back to Florida and wanted me to come with him.

Of course, my inner child had latched onto him, despite the red flags. I thought making sacrifices was what love was. I told myself that I loved him enough to give him everything, and I believed he would do the same for me if I asked him.

I see now that I was simply avoiding healing my childhood trauma and seeking validation, hoping that marrying this man would fill the void in my heart.

Across the world, we find this fantasy version of love celebrated: two lives coming together as one despite the odds. But does it always stay this way over time? Let's dive deeper into the perception of love.

Exercise Five: Setting Expectations in Your Relationships

In your companion journal, or on a separate sheet of paper, detail what unconditional love looks like for you. What things would you do if you loved yourself unconditionally? What would you need to let go of in order to achieve this vision of unconditional love?

CHOOSING A PARTNER

Love is complicated and often defies logic. Why do we fall in love at all? Is it out of necessity when we feel we're ready to start a family, or is there some chemical reaction in our brains that makes us fall in love?

All of us feel some form of vacancy in our hearts and have a strong desire to feel complete. We seek out love to replicate a feeling of warmth and closeness, so we can feel desired and wanted. And yes, our relationships with our parents contributes to how we choose romantic partners and become attached to other people. So, for example, if one of your parents has a very controlling personality, you're more likely to wind up in a dependent relationship.

My mother, an emotional but controlling person, decided everything for us. Therefore, it's not surprising that when I accepted my ex-husband's proposal, I did so because I'd been desperate for someone to depend on and wanted to go back to letting someone else make my decisions for me. Just like he didn't ask me to marry him—he decided I would marry him, and I went along with it because—in part—I'd always done what others told me to do. I didn't trust myself to make decisions. In many ways, I didn't even know how!

The same way someone with a victim mindset will continuously find themselves in relationships with abusive partners.

When we fall in love, we hardly think about what is "best" for us; we are more concerned with what feels familiar and welcoming. A sensitivity to attachment consumes and drives our love lives. This is why even when you feel miserable or vulnerable in a relationship, you have a hard time letting go and accepting that it's over.

We grow up seeing these romantic movies, becoming consumed by them, and imagine what we just saw for ourselves. And although there are times when a romantic movie has helped us to focus on the more touching aspects of humanity like love, trust, and hope. Often, the theme of romantic movies, especially the fairy tales we indulged in during our childhood and adolescence, doesn't match up with reality.

Instead, they were tools to condition us, especially women, to ascertain suitable and respectable gender roles, encouraging toxic behaviors like stalking and cat-calling, or emotional abuse. It's pollution to our minds really when you consider the storyteller's job is to feed us far-fetched, and, if analyzed, overly simplistic love affairs. But we continue to fantasize about this for ourselves.

Take, for example, the storyline for most romantic comedies.

The woman is typically second-class. She requires a man to save and protect her, not only from "the bad guy" but also from herself. As if she is incapable of making smart decisions and taking care of herself.

(Sound familiar?) Her lover is usually very charming, though a bit obsessive, as if he doesn't have his own group of friends or social life, infringing on her identity.

According to Jungian philosophy, in the process of self-discovery, there's a balance between our masculine (assertive) and feminine (passive) selves. However, society teaches women that obedience, subservience, and self-sacrifice are the keys to being worthy. Meanwhile, men are taught that they must be physically strong, wealthy and witty to be valued.

But we don't stop to think, as most young people won't today, how unreal these fictional fights and love-making really is when we're watching a movie. Today's "reality" shows are just as bad.

It's truly difficult to rid our minds of these storylines. Long after we've finished watching the movie, the formula the movie directors and writers used to make us laugh or cry still intoxicates and influences us. We don't realize how much we've bought into what we've been sold.

As a result, we carry these unrealistic expectations to our bed and in our hearts. We allow the entertainers that are there to amuse us, to shape our love lives; we start to believe this is what relationships should look like, how we should talk when we want to be romantic, and what we must do to find love. Only, real life doesn't follow movie scripts.

We have all heard about *love at first sight,* whether you believe it or not. We have also heard that "true" love lasts forever. In reality though, we fall in and out of love many times. But why? What is it about love that comes in uninvited, only to fade later on? Let's examine that through the various types of love.

TYPES OF LOVE

You may not experience all these types of love in your lifetime. Your first love may be your lasting love. Or, your soulmate may suddenly sweep you off your feet before you've had a chance to even process what's happening. But if you choose to open your heart to love, you will have the option of committing yourself to at least one of these three kinds of love:

First Love

When we're very young, we feel the first prick of Cupid's arrow even though we're not yet fully aware of our mind, body, or senses. We fall in love, sometimes secretly, scared to reveal such feelings, fearing they will be seen as lame.

This is the kind of love that is promoted by society. Its components are similar to the fairy tales we read or saw as children. It begins with the idea that this person is the perfect one for us. We should be humble, reserved and shy. There should be romance, sparks and butterflies, for this is our ride or die, and the success of this relationship hinges on us.

And if it doesn't make us feel good, or if our personal worth gets diminished, we overlook it because we think this is a part of being in love. In fact, we convince ourselves what we are experiencing is a part of true love. We ignore (or try to ignore) any red flags and bad behavior from our partner because we feel like–if we're just patient and try harder–everything will turn out right and that "love will conquer all", with a big, happy-ever-after.

Which is exactly why I was so willing to overlook anything that seemed wrong about my fiancé's attitudes and expectations. It wasn't him who was at fault, it was me. I needed to change. I needed to give him what he demanded, and then everything would work out just like it did in the movies.

In these first serious relationships, we tend to emphasize how our significant other feels about us rather than focusing on how we feel about them. That's how our family and society has taught us to evaluate our worth.

Because of this, our first love rarely works out. It feels exhilarating when we fall in love, but the initial enthusiasm soon wears off, and their flaws come in plain sight. Our horizons are just opening up, we start making future plans, and many of us decide to move to a new place to pursue our education or career. And we get tired of viewing the world through rose-colored glasses, and differences become irreconcilable when we lack the maturity and perspective necessary to sustain the relationship.

But our personal development continues. We build new habits, find interests more aligned with what we truly desire, and evolve. It is a learning experience that teaches us who we are, what our priorities are, and what we need out of a relationship.

This is the beginning of the second part of our love stories, the phase of "hard love."

The Melodramatic Love

Our second love is more powerful. We feel the pains of lies, deceptions, and insincerity more intensely. This is the kind of love that hurts.

Each time we fall in this kind of love, we imagine we'll make different choices, but in reality, we still subject ourselves to learning life's lessons the hard way. We find the rollercoaster of highs and lows addicting, and commit to writing a "unique" love story that pays tribute to endurance, rather than examining to see if the story we're creating in our minds matches the reality of it. We fail to ask if what we're engaged in is one of love at all.

We choose our romantic partners because "they make us laugh," "they know us better than we know ourselves," or "they're strong and independent." So even though the names of our partners change, and they wear different clothes, or travel in different circles, they will all fit the same mold.

It's not until we break the cycle of imagining "The One" do we make any real progress in selecting sustainable partners based on more reliable and unchanging characteristics. Until then, we keep replicating our interactions, thinking this time will be better than the last. And this is true for both women and men.

A guy friend of mine was once in love with a somewhat traditional Ethiopian girl. She was ambitious, smart, beautiful, and a free thinker.

He was swept away by her charm and thought she was the perfect woman to introduce to his family. I recall him saying he'd "never been happier" with anyone else.

Blinded by love, or maybe lust, he was unable to see that she was also emotionally unstable and vindictive. While they were out with friends she would try to make him jealous by flirting with other men and giving him the silent treatment. Even worse, she turned him against his best friends, wanting to keep his attention solely on her.

After a while he grew tired of being abused. Their relationship continued for about a year before he finally came to terms with who she really was really, and ended things. Her immaturity, games and disrespect were just too much to tolerate.

When you're selfless, giving as much as possible, with a partner that is inconsiderate, taking all that you offer—and then some—this kind of love is hurtful, confusing, and unhealthy. How many times have you allowed your partner to cry on you shoulders? And, how many times has it been reciprocated? In these situations, we give our hearts away thoughtlessly and perhaps too carelessly.

Abuse can be physical, but it can also be emotional, as it was in my case and my friend's case. And sometimes it's both. When you're in this kind of relationship, you'll find yourself feeling confused. What keeps us rooted in this kind of love? Is it our desire to want to "fix" someone or something, or fear of what's next?

Whether we're hooked on the passion and drama, or the state of our lives prevents us from doing something different is difficult to say, but trying to make our love affair last becomes our most important priority.

But as long as we continue to waste our time and energy preoccupied with this kind of disruptive love, we will continue to suffer. Even after it has ended, in the darkest and most secret corners of our hearts and minds we will prevent ourselves from learning from our past by wishing that the relationship could have lasted instead of letting go.

It takes a long time to get over this kind of love. But eventually, the rose-colored glasses come off, just like they did for me and my friend. Thankfully, our hearts ultimately reconciled what our minds had known all along—we deserve better.

The Unconditional Love

We don't notice it coming. We are too busy tending to our broken hearts or pretending we want to remain single forever. After past promises were made and broken, it feels as if we may not be able, or have no desire, to fall in love again. We feel safe relegating ourselves to a corner, relying on ourselves, and not subjecting ourselves to more heartache. But somehow, you still get noticed by someone and somehow—this seems different.

By this time we're different too. After multiple—or maybe one, horribly hurtful—relationships, we recognize that love isn't a fairy tale. We accept life for what it is—uncertain. And, in that uncertainty, when a love comes along that appears both stable and sustainable even though we promised "never again", we take the chance.

Not only that, but our damaged selves want more than anything to heal our wounds. We long to feel desired, protected, and cared for. In the end, setting the proper boundaries and demanding the right things will provide us the type of life and love we need.

Unconditional love happens without much turmoil. We neither have to be on our guard nor do we have to be self-sacrificing. This kind of relationship is born out of compassion and a matured outlook on what romance and love truly mean. The connection that is forged is more grounded and authentic, and although its cliche, it always seems to happen when we least expect it to.

It happens because we no longer have unrealistic expectations or a compulsion to be someone we're not. We can just be ourselves and not be judged for it, allowing the relationship to progress easily.

We were not looking for this kind of love because the fairy tales and the idealistic romantic novels we read didn't offer these kinds of scenarios. Before, we had to mold ourselves into a specific type of person to be accepted and loved. But, this kind of love shatters all our preconceived notions about relationships, offering unconditional love where we feel safe and find acceptance being ourselves.

It may take a while for this kind of love to reach our doorstep, but it's possible we aren't mentally or emotionally prepared to receive it.

When this type of love arrives, we may choose to ignore it, believing it's boring, or because we want to protect ourselves from more pain. But unconditional love is consistent, patiently waiting for us to consider it, notice it, and ultimately embrace it, helping us to grow and recognize what love really means—acceptance and recognition, mutual respect and companionship—harmony.

While our first love may be sweet. It may work. It may not. Our second love ix a storm, causing us to fight like enemies, trying to rip each other apart. But our third love, it is the most special because it helps both individuals thrive and find peace. No one forces us to accept this kind of love; it is not a compulsion. We choose to fall in love again because we want to.

WHY WE REPEAT TOXIC AFFAIRS

We also choose to love again because human beings are made to connect and be sociable. All of us long for a significant other and it truly does seem as though we're incomplete, somehow, without them. Some people try to fill that void with multiple relationships or careers or any number of things, but most of us keep looking for that other person to complete us.

Unfortunately, what's good for us isn't always what we look for in our other half. But, why is that? The answer lies in our childhood emotional experiences.

Some parents made their children believe they were the only ones who would love them. Others told their children they loved them, then mistreated them or neglected them causing conflict and a sense of mistrust. And most of us—in the best of circumstances, anyway—grow up believing no one in the world can accept or acknowledge us like our mom or dad.

That insecurity is responsible for what's reflected in your mind when you fall in love, making you passive and too understanding or dismissive of negative behavior. Because of this, someone taking advantage of you could also feel like this is acceptable or normal.

But the cruelty and bullying mixed with loving words and affection will make you believe it's worth enduring. There will be moments of happiness, closeness, and at times softness because a relationship can't be abusive all the time. Abusers work in a cycle: first they're kind, then they're toxic, and finally they're apologetic and promise that they'll never do that again; we forgive them because they seem so remorseful and sincere. And for a while all is good; so much so, we almost don't recognize or believe when the cycle starts to turn toxic again.

It is difficult to sort through such emotional turmoil and distress. Besides the familiarity of the relationship—and the time invested in it—prevents you from ending things. You wonder, "What will I do without their love anymore?" or worse, "What if they're right? What if I am unlovable and I'm the problem?" We are fearful, but also find ourselves feeling hopeful at times, so we stay.

Part of this is because the abuse is similar to the type of "love" we had as a child. We don't know any better. Often raised by narcissists, we suffered as children and could do nothing about it. Then as adults we seek the kind of situations we faced in our childhood, but now in our romantic relationships; often with the unconscious goal to come out on top (Lebow, *2021*). We duplicate our past hoping it will turn out right this time around.

But thankfully, we're not doomed to repeat these mistakes when we learn to recognize them. After walking the same path many times, we gather the wisdom to make better choices. We notice red flags, set boundaries, and learn from our pitfalls.

Then finally, we are ready for the love which may not look like what we were dreaming of, because we we were always looking for the wrong kind of love.

HOW TO RESCUE OURSELVES FROM DESTRUCTIVE LOVE

The French, known to be romantics, believe that love is a means to reach beyond ourselves. Plato, the philosopher, mentioned that love makes us whole again. The German philosopher Schopenhauer said love was a trick to make babies. The British philosopher Russell thought love was an escape from loneliness (*Asad, 2020*).

They all have a point; love is so much, but it is clearly not some things too.

It is not always a comfortable decision to leave a toxic relationship. Such love damages not only our minds but also our body. This is a precise representation of our emotional and mental health.

It reveals itself as an upset stomach, a loss of appetite, muscle pains and aches, dizziness and headaches, restless nights, cold sweats, a racing heart, rising blood pressure, and more. This creates stress, anxiety, and depression.

We rescue ourselves from the clutches of destructive love by stopping it right in its tracks. That involves reflecting on our past, finding the connections between different events, and rationally analyzing why we constantly make the same choices.

Ask yourself:

- What pain did I endure due to my loved ones?
- What are the repetitive mistakes I am making in my relationships? In what ways have my partners been similar?
- Am I looking at my relationships through rose colored glasses, hoping they will get better or change? Am I looking for them to fix past hurts?
- What qualities of my parents or caregivers did I put up with as a child? Which do I cherish most?
- Am I repeating habits that I was forced to live through when I was a child?
- Am I rejecting or accommodating people who have similar characteristics as those who've previously tormented me while pretending to be unaffected by my past?

If you are in this kind of relationship, consider taking a break and find a space where you can think quietly and logically. Maybe even, discover ways to survive on your own. Seek professional help to guide you.

Exercise Six: Feeling Secure in Your Romantic Relationships

In your companion journal or on a separate sheet of paper describe what have your past relationships taught you about what you do and do not want in a life partner? What do you need in a romantic relationship to feel loved? What do you require from your partner to have your needs and wants met? What boundaries will you need to set to feel safe and secure?

IS THIS LOVE?

Looking to escape to all the wrong places.

Torturing myself in pitch black places.

Is this love?

Nothings the same when you're coasting

Or as I like to say, chasing

Looking for that one thing, something, anything

And now I'm off, wander-lusting

Searching for a high just as good as the last

And when equal to isn't enough, better than becomes the only thing I'll have

Aspiring to transcend higher

Beyond anything I could have hoped for

Subtly anxious, extremely nervous

Deeply afraid of being disappointed

Subconsciously building excitement that my every dream might finally be

The highest of all highs that will make all the lows worthwhile

Not just the bad trips and low blows, but life and thereafter

Because if this is it, the highest high, I won't allow it to evade me

After all, I'd gladly die if I knew you, my love, was waiting for me on the other side

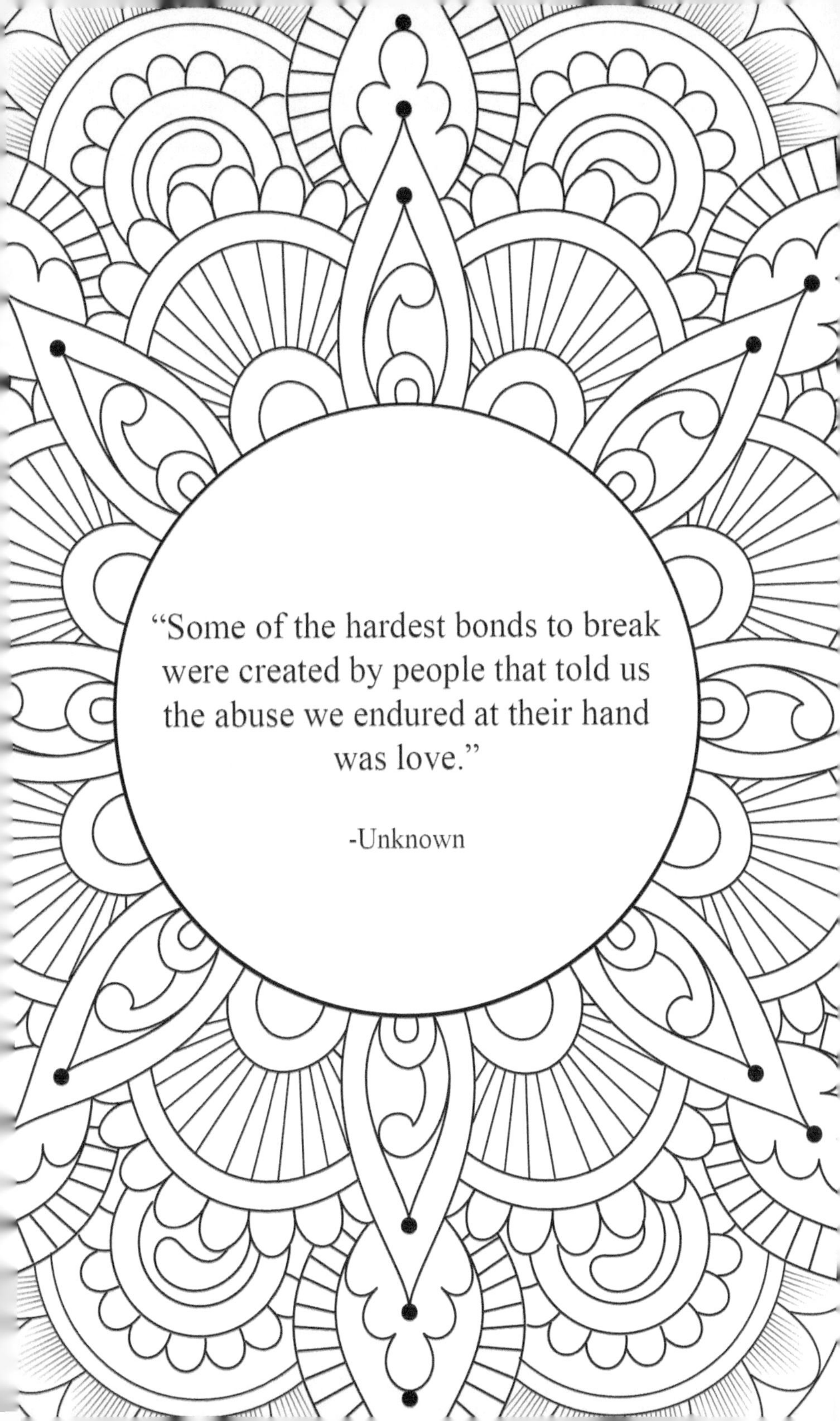

"Some of the hardest bonds to break were created by people that told us the abuse we endured at their hand was love."

-Unknown

Chapter Five

THE RELATIONSHIP SHOULD'VE NEVER BEEN

SOMEHOW, my future ex-husband convinced me that moving to his hometown, Orlando, would be good for us. He argued that it would benefit his music career, but also my modeling career. So, I saved up to help him get us a place.

The plan was to be living in a place of our own in perfect harmony by the end of the school year. He would arrive in Florida several months before me to get things settled while I finished out the semester at school. That was the goal.

And at the time it seemed like a solid plan. I was in my second year of college, working tirelessly; I had a job in the financial aid office and was modeling on the side. Despite the relationships I'd built, I still felt very much alone.

Then right before the end of my sophomore year, there was in an incident that forced our plans to change. I was being stalked by someone who knew where I lived, went to school, and worked. The police believed it was someone that had followed me home after working a modeling gig, but was never able to do anything about it. Needless to say I no longer felt safe, so I left my apartment and went to stay with my mom.

I took the opportunity to reveal to her I was moving and because I didn't feel safe returning to my apartment, I was moving sooner than I'd originally planned. Within a couple weeks my apartment was packed, I'd shipped my things off and arranged to take my finals out in Florida.

When I first arrived, I was thrilled to begin this exciting new adventure with the man I loved. I'd helped him find our joint residence inside a gated community, and was pleased with the progress he'd made furnishing and decorating the place before my arrival. But the enthusiasm was short-lived as the plan for my life started to fall apart.

Shortly after arriving, I discovered my financial aid wouldn't transfer. According to the state of Florida, I was no longer "need based" which disqualified me for the academic scholarship. I agreed it wouldn't be wise to rake up a bunch of debt, so my degree would have to wait until we saved up enough money for me to afford to continue my education.

My modeling career also fizzled out after a too-good-to be-true opportunity from what seemed like a legitimate agency popped up on my radar. All was going well initially, however when I was late for a callback because I was unable to leave work early, we discovered the agency was a scam. Within a week's time their office had disappeared—along with my entire portfolio and life's work.

It was after I was left with very little to keep me busy that I noticed my connection with my fiancé hadn't grown. Quite the opposite, it'd become tense and uncomfortable. I felt as if I was always walking on eggshells.

Prior to moving, I'd fantasized about date nights and what it'd be like to finally share a bed. To fall asleep in each other's arms and wake up to one another every day. I imagined all these blissful moments and complete contentment. But that was a far cry from reality.

Actually, we worked opposite schedules, so we rarely saw one another. And on the rare occasions when I'd stay awake waiting for him, he'd come home only to close himself off in another room to play video games or make music, leaving me to my own devices.

Despite our family's traditions he despised consumerism connected to the celebration of pagan holidays, though being in hospitality he worked most holidays anyway. Additionally, he claimed romance was "not his thing." I can count the number of times I received flowers on one hand. Ultimately, he made sure to let me know I would have to get used to going without.

In this new environment, I felt even more alone than before and our relationship lacked intimacy because of it. But what hurt more than anything was what I felt was a lack of effort. He did the absolute bare minimum and expected me to accept it. For instance, I recall celebrating our one-year anniversary at Chipotle. Although I'd grown up eating there and was still constantly eating at he fast-food chain, internally, I was appalled by his choice of restaurant for such a significant occasion. We dined at the restaurant in some of our nicest clothes and made the best of it, but it was those kinds of incidents that made me feel undervalued.

Therefore, my resentment grew. This caused us to argue more, and when we argued it was like he'd become a different person, like Dr. Jeckyll and Mr. Hyde. He would say vile things, worse than anything anyone had ever said to me in my life, and he was extremely aggressive. I recall a specific incident where he got so mad he punched a hole in the wall during one of our arguments, then fixed it the next day as if it was nothing.

It didn't take long for me to shut down, which in return made him angrier. In hindsight I realize that talking with a therapist before my move, or even after I arrived in Florida, to express my fears and worries instead of pretending like they didn't exist, would have benefited me. Doing so would have helped to manage my expectations, enjoy this new chapter, and reinforce my own self-worth. But, I didn't. Instead, I repressed my emotions and isolated myself, too ashamed to tell friends and family the details of my circumstances.

Meanwhile my fiancé assured me this was just an adjustment period. This was the first "real" relationship he'd been in, and he'd never shared his space with anyone before.

Still, he regularly vocalized how much I was crowding his space and being too clingy and needy. He told me I could no longer go to any sports events with him because they weren't enjoyable when I was around because I would cheer for the opposing team on occasion. He went so far as to tell me to "get a life" because he couldn't be my whole world.

Even though he did little to show me he cared, he still demanded certain things from me. I worked full-time and was expected to take care of home in meticulous ways, like hand-washing the dishes the way he preferred. Still, the extra effort on my part failed to please him.

Instead, he appeared to relish making me feel small every chance he could; this went on day after day. His hurtful words stuck with me even when I tried to make friends and adjust to this new life, poisoning my happiness and fueling my anxiety and stress.

Here I was, in a state where I knew no one, and my fiancé was telling me, in so many words, that he was unhappy with our relationship. Worse, he made me feel selfish for wanting to spend time with him.

Without considering all his expectations for me, he'd never even visited my hometown to see where I grew up or even to meet my family despite how often I returned home. He'd consistently say that he felt as if he could never make me happy and was overwhelmed by trying.

But I had dropped out of school and moved to the opposite side of the country to be with him, and even stayed with him after I'd caught him lying and cheating. I wasn't sure what more I could do.

I thought back to the words my mother wrote in my yearbook, "Finally, the day has come for you to move out... Oh, I mean move on and become even more successful than you've been. You've come a long way transferring from school to school until finding this one. I think we set a record of four years at one school! But look at you, all grown up and ready for college, and I'm sure you'll be just fine. We love you and wish you the best."

I didn't want to return home, tail between my legs. I had to figure out how to make it work. I had to stay in Florida.

Was I too prideful to admit I was wrong about him? Was I embarrassed? I honestly can't say. But instead of thinking about what was best for me, I decided it was more important to not fail, and put all my energy into trying to make things easier for him, hoping things would get better for me.

Even after my disappointment and inability to please the man I loved, and despite the many red flags, we got married two years after I'd arrived in Florida. I was a twenty-one, almost twenty-two-year-old, hopeless romantic who had taken a leap of faith and risked it all for love.

It was just like those romantic comedies I'd watched. My new husband was adamant that he would always be honest with me, even if it hurt my feelings, and vowed to communicate his own feelings more openly. I naively believed that once we were married things would get better. But just like moving to Florida, being a wife was nothing like the fairy tale role I imagined it would be.

Feb. 4, 2011

I've missed my husband. Our time together this weekend was great. I want to be back in the same bed but our bedroom is now a trigger—waiting for him to come home, or wanting him to spend time with me when he wants to sleep is just too depressing. It keeps me up at night even when he's not here. I naturally wake up around midnight hoping to see him when he gets in. But 12:15am comes and goes, and as it gets later and later and he still isn't home I find myself getting angry. Looking ahead feels like a long and tiresome road. I don't know if I can make it. But I try to remember how far we've come and embrace the challenges as they come. Breaking my habit of thinking negatively has been difficult and I find myself harming myself every day. But I know it's a process and I believe if I stay faithful and strong, I will prevail.

I could see he was trying to change, and although ultimately it wasn't enough, at the time I chose to see it as progress and preferred not to nag him, thinking it would help. I did everything I could to not rock the boat. But instead of my acceptance bringing him closer to me, he used the time and space to begin engaging with other women, even more so than before. He entertained and flirted with his employees so much that someone filed a third-party sexual harassment claim with human resources because his interactions made them feel so uncomfortable.

Once again, I did nothing out of fear of making things worse. Instead, I withdrew further, not standing up for myself, letting him disrespect me and our relationship. I'd simply grown tired of asking him to love and respect me.

I prayed for a sign, asking God if I should return to Colorado, or stay in Florida because what was happening in my marriage just made me so unhappy. I didn't feel loved, and felt more depressed than ever.

But God was silent. So finally, I'd had enough and told my husband I wanted a divorce.

He responded by trying to physically throw me out of our apartment, along with my clothes that he yanked out of the closet after claiming I had ruined his life.

Less than a month later I found out I was pregnant; I took this as a sign that God wanted me to stay with my husband.

THE PAIN OF EMOTIONAL ABUSE

Emotional abuse leaves scars—you just can't see them. In a way, this makes it worse than physical abuse because people who love and care about you can't see how battered and bruised you are. No one truly knows except you and your abuser. As a result, victims stay silent, isolate themselves, and become secretive.

Emotional abuse is a type of suffering that has no specific definition, diagnosis, or treatment. You can take prescription drugs like antidepressants to elevate your mood, or minimize and mask your inner turmoil hoping it will go away. But the truth is, you feel stuck, and every living moment is heavy with pain. You don't live, you're simply surviving. And it can be miserable.

For some people falling in love is just a pastime. Their relationships include a few sweet words and sex, but they avoid responsibility and commitment. But is that not harmful to their partner emotionally? Have they not taken advantage of that person's acceptance and vulnerability? Sure. But, selfishly, abusers don't care.

After a while, I began to believe every word uttered by my husband was a lie and every promise he made was only going to be broken. Love and security, those things I once believed in so strongly, were mere myths, narratives created to masterfully possess and dominate my time and affection. Over time, I realized that I'd romanticized my relationship; and I finally accepted that I'd come in this world alone and would likely leave it the same way when the time came.

I was truly afraid of what the future held. Which led me to question, *is it possible to die of a broken heart?* Believe it or not, emotional stressors can bring on what doctors call "broken heart syndrome". Any significant loss—the death of a loved one, a divorce, or a loss of income—can actually "break" your heart. Although the exact cause of broken heart syndrome is unclear, researchers have determined that its symptoms can mimic those of a heart attack.

Essentially, I determined emotional pain could indeed kill me. So, if you've ever felt this way, know that you're not being dramatic; even if the people who claim to love you seem to enjoy telling you that you are.

It may be difficult for some people to understand that the pain of letting go of someone we love, even when violence is present, is just as hard to accept as if the relationship was perfect; despite the abuse, we will cling to the romance.

PHASES OF LOVE

There are three phases of love in every relationship: the honeymoon phase, the compatibility phase, and finally, the permanent phase.

The Honeymoon Phase

The honeymoon phase is defined by passion, lust and even giddiness. This is when new lovers become super-charged with New Relationship Energy (NRE), when we spend a lot of time discovering our significant other and don't care to focus on much of anything else. Our new partner seems perfect in every way.

The Compatibility Phase

Once the initial newness and desire of the honeymoon phase wears off, we begin to explore the compatibility between ourselves and our partner. We begin to ask ourselves, *Is my partner worthy (of me)?* Consequently, a mental tug-of-war between lovers follows to determine each other's position in the relationship and to establish who holds the power.

This period can lead to a lot of mental anguish. It can also lead to emotional torment, if–like me–you submit to your partner's demands in the misguided belief that challenging them means you'll lose their love. This is where those romantic comedies mislead us because those characters will preserve through their challenges proving their love is true.

But true love means compromising and a willingness to understand one another's perspectives. It should be based on your strengths and honesty. Neither partner should want to win over the other, or play these types of games when it comes to matters of the heart.

You can best get through the compatibility phase of love through open communication and by working out your conflicts. If you're not sure of the relationship, consider taking a break to think logically about the connection you share with your partner. Look at the bigger picture and visualize your future with this person. And be honest! Will you truly be happy? Does your partner have your best interest in mind?

If you're naive like I was, you will probably make the same mistake I did during this phase. I expected a happily-ever-after when I should have acknowledged my doubts about our incompatibility. Failing to do so will result in unbalanced and unhealthy relationship from both you and your partner's perspective.

The Permanent Phase

After you have settled the power struggles and identity crises, you arrive at the permanent phase. Here, the crucial word that helps your love move forward is "patience." Couples who love each other fight and complain, but they are always patient and tolerant of one another. And although the word tolerate gets a bad rap, it simply means to accept or endure something or someone with patience, self-control or restraint. It is the commitment to the relationship and each other that keeps the love alive (*Beasley*, *2021*).

This type of commitment allows your love to thrive because you can freely work through the ups and downs of the relationship. There will be days when you get irritated by your partner, and there will be days when you feel that you can't live without them. Both can be true.

And if you are in a relationship that heals, supports, and nurtures you, you must fight for it! Your relationship doesn't have to be difficult or full of conflict. If you feel unloved at times you must move beyond the emotional abuse you tolerated in the past or grown up with; accept that it brought you enlightenment and experience, and the understanding that you are worthy of respect and love simply because you were born.

Do not feel guilt, anger, or remorse over what happened. If anything, it brought you where you stand today.

On the other hand, our almost-willing participation in abusive relations makes me ask: *Are we negligent when it comes to caring for ourselves? Do we receive any kind of satisfaction from remaining in denial or staying with someone who is abusive towards us? And how does the abuse affect us mentally, emotionally and physically?*

There may be many reasons we cling to a relationship despite being abused, including: financial security, the need for companionship, or it may be simply psychological. After all, it is all in the name of love.

We sought love in our childhood, trying to get it from our parents, siblings, and relations. *Love* meant *acceptance*.

But in the face of abuse, we must accept that there is no love, not truly.

In the end, there's no use in asking yourself how or why this happened to you. The situation evolved over time, without our even noticing. However, the moment we recognize for what it is we have no choice we must move on.

Your story, unlike mine, may not be about a husband. But, replace the husband with a friend, a partner, or even a family member, and you'll get the same response.

The main thing is, if we are to be at peace and find love within ourselves, we need to forgive. Because in order to truly move forward and fall in love we cannot hate the experiences that shaped us.

Let us look a little deeper into what it's like to embrace the right kind of love.

EMBRACING THE RIGHT RELATIONSHIP

We've heard about love and marriage our whole lives and how amazing it can be. By design, we are meant to connect with others and face the world with someone who will be supportive and caring—someone we can receive from and also give to.

Nowadays a lot of people are only willing to engage in sexual relationships, frightened by the intimacy of being vulnerable with someone, afraid of failing, or being abandoned in love; these individuals are what we call "commitment-phobes." And those that are afraid to commit will also be reluctant to give the required time, patience, and effort a romantic relationship demands.

Yet, so many of us are unaware of how we should *feel* when in love, which makes identifying someone afraid of commitment very difficult.

Psychologists say we ultimately find our one true love when we are no longer lost, or in transition, and are ready for partnership and mutual understanding. But, how will we know when have arrived at that point?

It is hard to describe love and how you should feel when you are in love because the language of love is different for everyone. You can make compromises in the relationship, going without quality time and find comfort in your significant other's words or extravagant gifts instead; but if words don't mean much to you and you're not a material person, those things will never be enough. Everyone has things that will make them feel loved, desired, and secure; love languages are different for each of us. But one thing is for certain—you should be reminded of your value when you look into your spouse's eyes.

For some, love is still selfish—as humans we oftentimes desire to be loved before we are ready to trust and give our love to someone else. But love should not be one-sided. It is a connection between two people from different walks of life ,with diverse backgrounds and various triggers. Both individuals need to feel seen and heard by their partner.

If you think about it, love is a verb—an action—not a noun (or an emotion). Real, true love is also unconditional. "Unconditional" means unquestioning, unchanging, wholehearted and complete. If your love is unconditional, you won't make decisions based solely on your own interest, keep score, or place blame.

However, if you have found your true love, someone who makes you feel appreciated, safe and cared for—hold on to them. You may think someone better will potentially come along, but love doesn't happen like that. As Anna in the British television program, *Downton Abbey*, once said, "...it is not a bus that comes every ten minutes."

Love is not like going shopping. You might dream of having a rich and sexy partner, but those details are not really important in the grand scheme of things. Lasting love requires three fundamental factors: mutual trust, respect and understanding. Your significant other could be a millionaire or a sanitation worker, but it is those three essential components that will ensure your partnership withstands the test of time.

SELF-LOVE IN A RELATIONSHIP

While being in love with someone else is great, it is important to also love yourself freely and unconditionally to strengthen your empathy, improve your decision-making skills, and maintain your emotional, mental, and spiritual health. When you love yourself, you develop self-compassion. By showing kindness to yourself, you let go of your guilt and forgive your past mistakes, you start paving the road to your future with self-preservation and healing.

If you've been through emotional trauma, use that as fuel to ignite your mind with a passion for self-awareness and self-love. Learn to accept yourself for who you are, and find a way to move beyond your past pain and suffering. Healing may come later rather than sooner, but it will come. And before you know it, you will have made it through to the other side.

Exercise Seven: Letting Go of The Past

In your companion journal, or on a separate sheet of paper, write down what you would need to let go of in order to make room for the ideal partner to come into your life? How would you need to grow and develop yourself in order to be ready for the healthy relationship and lasting love that this partner would bring?

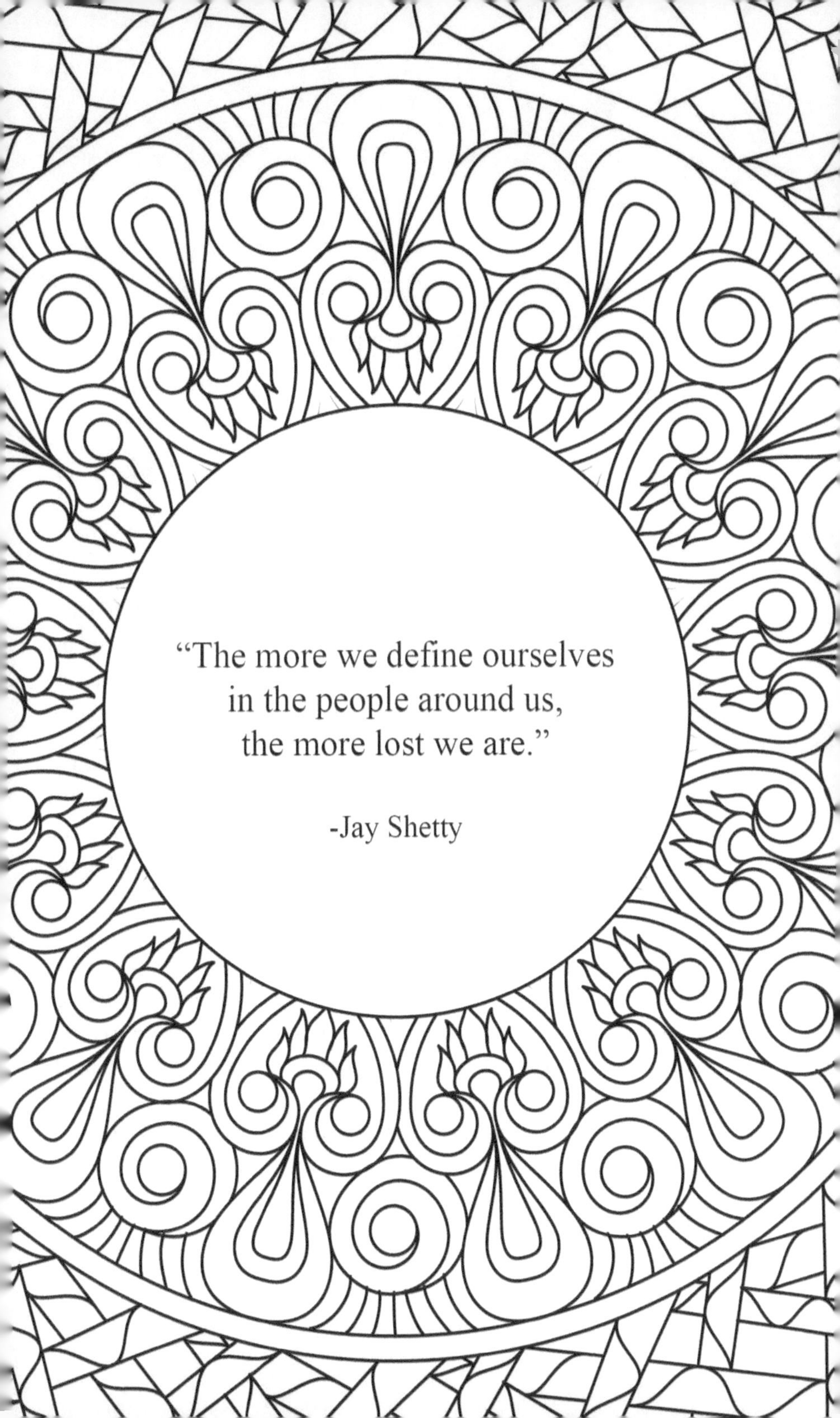

"The more we define ourselves
in the people around us,
the more lost we are."

-Jay Shetty

Chapter Six

FEELING LOST

FOR NINE MONTHS and three weeks, I numbed myself as much as I could after I found out I was pregnant. I desperately wanted my marriage to work. I reminded myself that everything I felt during pregnancy would be felt by our unborn child.

As always, I was trapped in the delusion of "as soon as...", "when..." and "after...". Once again, I thought things would be different—after I gave birth. So I focused on pouring all my love into someone who needed it—our son. I was convinced that he would fill the void in my heart.

Jan. 12, 2013

It's been a while. I figured writing again might help me mentally and emotionally get through some of the things that have left me broken. The year of 2012 wasn't great, but there are some things that happened that deeply affected me, especially giving birth to Carter. It was everything. I live and breathe for him. My husband also ended the year leaving me feeling betrayed and disappointed. But I won't get into why, too many angry emotions tied to that – which is why I'm journaling. I guess I only do this when things get really bad and as they get better I disappear.

Well I am going to try to: one, continuously write, two, write more positive than negative, and three, evolve. Carter has magnified my desire to be a better person. But with all that's been happening I know I can't be a good wife unless my husband is good to me, and although I believe in 'faking it until you make it', for the sake of everyone's happiness, progress needs to be made. I believe my husband is capable of change, and being everything I want him to be. I believe he wants to be this as well, but instead he allows other things to get in the way of this goal. So maybe he won't change, or maybe it will be too late when he finally does.

This is my dilemma.

WHY DO WE FEEL LOST IN LIFE?

The explanation for feeling lost is not cut and dry. Some of us are grounded, while some of us live inside our minds constantly analyzing and worrying, reflecting on the past or thinking about our futures—expecting someone else to make us feel happy or secure. But still, even those who live in the moment are not always in the best headspace. They find themselves dissatisfied even when they have loving, supportive people in their life that are sympathetic from the get-go. Instead they tend to push people away, preferring to bury themselves in self-pity, not wanting to rely on anyone.

But why?

Why are so many people walking around miserable on the inside? Why does operating on auto-pilot, minimizing our emotions still cause us to be unhappy? This can be caused by things like job dissatisfaction, lack of friends, or questioning how their life ended up a certain way.

In these types of situations, we tend to feel like life serves no real meaning therefore we feel like we have no purpose. Every day is a replay of the previous day; relationships and money are a struggle, and people constantly give you the same advice: workout, eat healthier, take better care of yourself. But when we feel hopeless, doing these things won't provide an escape from what feels like a distressing life.

We accept this as our fate, thinking, "it could be worse" and seem to keep grinding.

In my opinion, the leading cause for this, even before the coronavirus pandemic, is the overwhelming chaos within our lives—from our work, relationships, emotions, and obligations. We all are struggling with commitments, constraints, and constant demands.

We're all disconnected from personal interaction, although we're connected by things such as social media. Social interaction has become virtual instead of tangible, robotic instead of natural. This sort of detachment has caused mental, emotional and spiritual fatigue.

Honestly, my therapist used to be the only person I really talked to, who gave me dedicated time. She sat with me and listened to my problems. She was the one I could talk to about whatever was happening in my life without reservation. She had an open-minded attitude and gave suggestions and new perspectives so that I could look beyond my emotional pain, anxiety, worries, and fears.

Years ago, back before we became so "busy", and people lived in the here and now instead of living at a distance or in solitude, our "therapists" were our sincerest friends, neighbors, and wise family members who put blood first, no matter what.

The hyperconnectivity in digital environments, thanks to the internet and social media, has fogged our minds. Our brain are not designed to constantly handle the gazillions of miscellaneous snippets that pass through it everyday. With so much information for us to process, it's no wonder we feel distracted and lost.

Am I making smart decisions? Am I taking care of myself? Or doing what's right for my loved ones? Questions like this trouble our minds without interruption, even when we try to distract ourselves with entertainment, causing us to truly feel lost.

The sheer volume of information provided to us by news feeds, emails, DMs, television series and texts is detrimental to our mental and emotional health. We remain confused by the contradictory information poured into our minds and have a hard time concentrating on any one meaningful and concrete solution that will help us successfully attain what it is we set out to accomplish.

FEELING MORE IN CONTROL

Our tendency to work towards perfection is by design. What is "perfect" has been carefully painted and portrayed by the media for generations, circulated, and embedded in our minds, deciding how we should be valued. Even now, on social media, not only are we measuring our worth by the numbers of followers and likes, but we are also voluntarily engaging in a game of "keeping up with the Joneses," displaying only our greatest achievements and successes for everyone to see.

The media and the elite keenly establish what we should buy to look attractive, which brands are deluxe and are therefore must-haves, the latest trends to follow, what cars mean that we have moved up in social status, etc.

When we are in pursuit of a false sense of satisfaction and success, we are gambling with our happiness. By going along with those that are superficial you'll find yourself constantly appraising your success based on the things you've acquired. The process is gradual at first, but eventually the desire for money and material possessions will dominate every aspect of your life. Not to mention, if you want to acquire more stuff, you must partake in the infamous rat race and dedicate less time and energy to things that you truly enjoy.

I believe most of the struggle is with ourselves. We're uncertain about what makes us truly happy and satisfied in life. We question our purpose and this can happen to anyone regardless of economic or social status.

To be happy, you must be at peace with yourself, not conflicted. Recognizing where you come from and who you are brings acceptance. And with acceptance comes freedom.

Instead of comparing your life to the next person's, measure your success based on what you want in *your life*. Whether that's a good family life, time to follow your passions, relaxation, opportunities to travel, reading good books and listening to music, or meaningful interactions. These are all fundamental sources of happiness we can pursue.

Accept ads, social media and streaming services for what they are: cunning marketing strategies businesses exploit to increase profits. I'm not saying don't treat yourself every once in a while. But you should also try to avoid getting carried away.

Find a way to ignore the many distractions that your smartphone's algorithm selects for you on a daily basis. Schedule time for each of your hobbies, and the things that are important to you. Allot time for each of them on different days of the week if you find you have limited availability. This way, you're squeezing in some self-care, and will get the most out of each day without becoming overwhelmed, frustrated or anxious by every little thing. Socialize with your friends from time to time.

Most importantly, find your purpose. Without a defined purpose, you will float aimlessly, letting life just happen to you. And although going with the flow may sound fun and easy, it's important to find yourself in the grand scheme of things. Doing this helps to connect the dots, provides reassurance and reveals what's in store for your future.

On the other hand, if you get distracted or become engrossed in the messiness of life, happiness will be out of your reach and your troubles will not melt away; they'll simply remain buried. To resolve your problems, you must challenge them. Try visualizing a more controlled and uncompromising you–your "higher self" if you will, and what that version of you might want out of life. Striving to be the best version of yourself will increase your self-worth.

There will be no need to seek validation and approval from other people for the things you do. Being happy with who you are will make you more content. And people will gravitate towards you because they know you are deeply in love with life.

And if you feel lost and alone, know that there are many like you; although people are often not outspoken about how they feel, everyone struggles with loneliness at some point. But, never forget it is a burden you can overcome. Everything has a reason behind it; if you are feeling lonely, then it's possible you need to spend some time self-reflecting.

It is important to have time for ourselves. Time is truly precious being that it's the only resource, free of cost, that we can't get back. So, even if you find yourself feeling discouraged and disappointed with life, let it not discourage you or diminish your self-worth. Do not surrender to the feelings of depression; instead, take advantage of the alone time.

And I know that's easier said than done, but it is possible. Perspectives change, and needs change. Therefore, people *can* change, including you.

Exercise Eight: Discovering Your Higher Self

In your companion journal, or on a separate sheet of paper, write a reverse bucket list of things that do not serve you that you're going to stop doing. What would it take for you to be kinder to yourself at this moment? What would it sound like if you spoke to yourself the way you would your best friend or a small child?

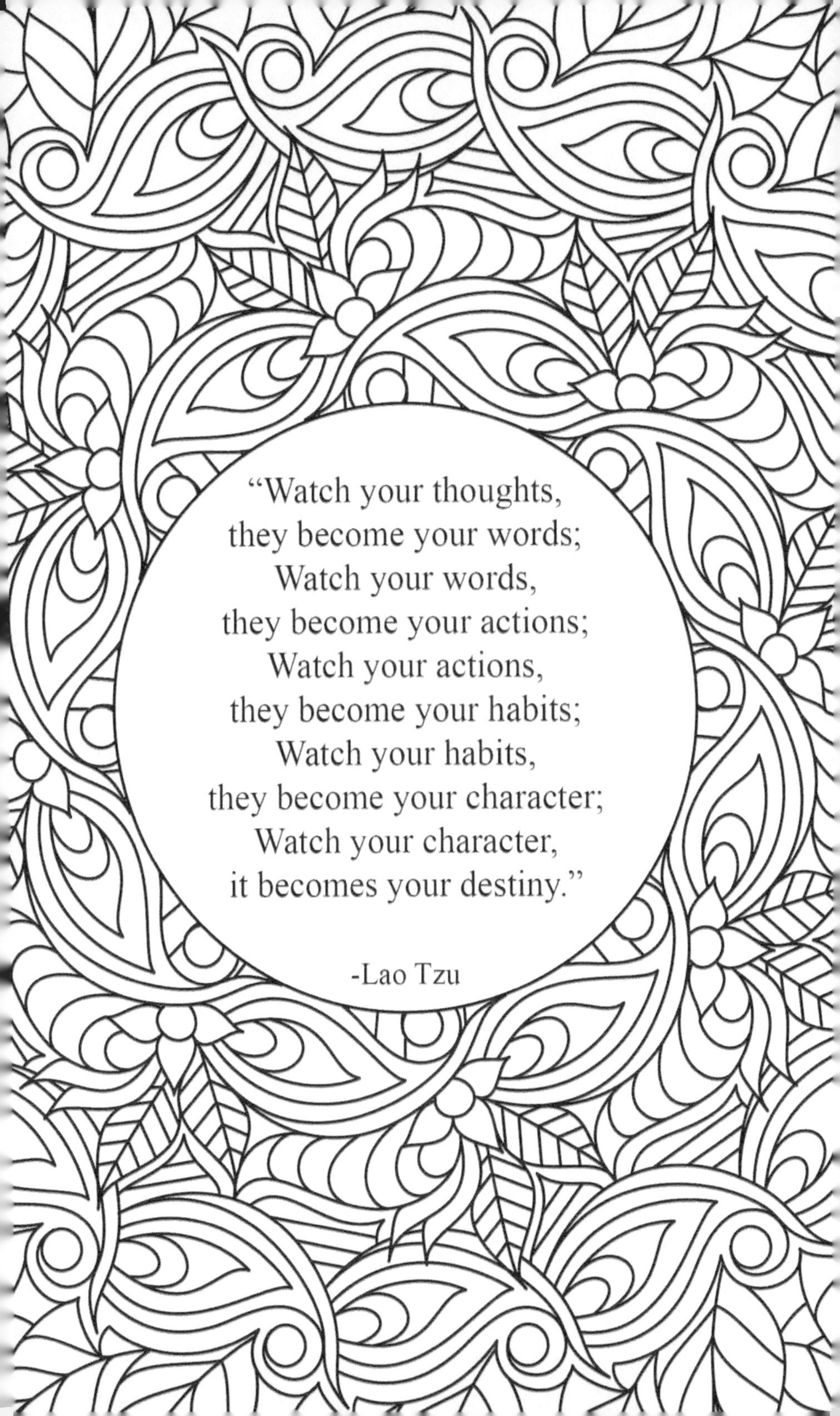

"Watch your thoughts,
they become your words;
Watch your words,
they become your actions;
Watch your actions,
they become your habits;
Watch your habits,
they become your character;
Watch your character,
it becomes your destiny."

-Lao Tzu

Chapter Seven

THE TUNNEL

WHILE DOING everything I could possibly think of to save my marriage, my body was physically shutting down. I was having hot flashes, I would get winded just from bathing or washing my hair, I had vivid nightmares, and even had dizzy spells. But it wasn't until I was on my way to work and rear-ended someone at a red light, after momentarily losing consciousness behind the wheel, that my husband stopped calling me a hypochondriac.

I went through many tests: stress tests, sleep tests, MRI's, CT scans, blood tests, EKGs, and a ton of other exams, only to be told there was physically nothing wrong with me. My primary physician was delivering the results of the latest test, which had come back normal when I broke down. As I cried and insisted the tests were wrong, she did her best to soothe me and as a last-ditch effort suggested we try a hormone test. I was desperate and willing to try anything. So, I gathered saliva samples and sent them to the lab where they determined that I was not producing the primary stress hormone called cortisol.

Cortisol is a steroid hormone released by your adrenal glands that regulates a wide range of vital processes throughout the body. It helps your body deal with stress, sadness, and anxiety. Think of it as your built-in alarm system, automatically triggered when you're in a situation your mind and body perceive as stressful or frightening.

It had been almost a year of testing and we finally had concrete results! By now I had been seeing this doctor for over five years and I'd grown to trust her. She knew my husband was unsupportive because he was never at any of the appointments, unless he was my ride home, and I the only time I talked about him was when I was defending his absence.

I shared with her a few of the things that were going on at home, and she explained it was important to reduce the amount of stress I was under and recommended I begin seeing a therapist again. I'd participated in some form of therapy while in high school and I knew it could help, but I wasn't really a fan of it.

Originally, I felt my therapist, whoever they might be, couldn't possibly understand what I'd endured. Like my therapist in high school, for example, constantly made me uncomfortable. She was always putting thoughts in my head that hadn't been there before, or ever really. But I was too young to understand her motives at the time.

However, on account of the latest test results, I knew the problem wasn't going to just fix itself. So, I approached my husband about couples therapy, and although it took a bit of convincing, we eventually began seeing a psychiatrist.

I understood my husband was the primary reason my health was suffering. I had become so fearful of him that we wrote notes to one another as if we were long-distance again to express our feelings because we couldn't get things resolved when we spoke face-to-face.

My sole purpose in asking him to go to therapy was to work on our communication. However, after two sessions, I discovered he'd had an affair while I was pregnant. He said she was just someone who made him feel desired, just a boost to his ego. However, after I'd listened to him tell me to take all the time I needed to heal, and that he'd be there no matter what, this caused me to lose faith in him entirely and completely shut down.

In a life-changing crisis that defies all logic and expectations, we find ourselves at a crossroad, often unable to handle what's in front of us. We implode, crushed by our sadness, grieving our hopes and dreams because we got something else instead.

Whether it is a family confrontation, a breakup, or the umpteenth relapse, it becomes impossible to sort through our emotions on our own. We simply do not have the fortitude to sort through everything to determine how to cope with this traumatic experience.

If you feel this way, it is time to seek professional help. And by help, I mean psychological treatment options like Cognitive Behavioral Therapy (CBT), Psychodynamic Therapy, Dialectical Behavior Therapy (DBT), or any alternative treatment option outside of psychiatric medication.

As people, we tend to hold ourselves back, relying on our imaginary safety net of security and love. We must be inspired and motivated to face our inner demons, but until we start to eliminate those, we can't understand the tremendous resourcefulness and wherewithal we have within ourselves. And as long as we envision ourselves as victims we can never muster up the courage to tap into those resources, therefore the cycle continues.

But it took some time for therapy to have a positive effect on me. Understandably so, considering my whole life was falling apart. The man I loved, and the father of my only child, was seeking affection in someone else's arms; it was more than I could stand.

I tried to naturally manage my stress for some time, but I eventually accepted her referral and went to see a psychiatrist who could prescribe something to help with the chemical imbalance in my brain, and a psychologist to provide a nonjudgmental, safe place to talk and help me sort through my feelings. The admission form included questions like, "over the past two weeks, how often have you had a poor appetite?" Or "have you had difficulty falling asleep or staying asleep?"

At the time I didn't know this was a depression screening used to classify individuals with a major depressive disorder. So I answered honestly, and with everything going on in my life my answers conveyed, absolutely without a shadow of a doubt, I was depressed.

However, when the psychologist sat me down and began asking more questions, I found myself getting defensive. Mostly because I felt like she was tiptoeing around the question she really wanted to ask, "Why don't you love yourself?" Instead, she asked questions like, "Are you eating three meals a day?", "Do you shower every day?", "Do you prefer to stay at home versus going out and being with friends or family?"

As I sat across from her and answered each question, I felt I was giving her reasons to think less of me, so I started to explain myself. I told her that I had moved across the country and had no family nearby and the only friends I had were people my husband had introduced me to. But after finding out he had been cheating with a coworker, who was also friends with someone I'd considered a friend and agreed to let live with us, I felt there was no one I could trust.

I didn't shower every day because who showers every single day if they haven't been anywhere and had no plans to go anywhere? I also didn't eat three meals a day because I was often too busy feeding my infant. But nothing I said made a difference. She insisted I would not find a solution to my problems unless I trusted the process. She said "If you want my help you have to be willing to accept the fact that you need to be here."

I wanted her to get to know me before diagnosing me with mental health issues. I believed I was simply in a really bad situation and needed help sorting out my feelings. But from her perspective, I was in denial, and in hindsight I was. I was afraid of what it meant to be diagnosed with a mental illness. I felt horrible, but again what else could I do?

So, I scheduled my next appointment on my way out and stopped by the pharmacy on my way home to pick up the medication the physiatrist had prescribed. Thus began my journey with therapy and anti-depressants.

IS THERAPY RIGHT FOR YOU?

Talking to a psychiatrist or a therapist has been proven to benefit 75% of participants.

It involves talking about your past connections, personal experiences, emotions, and what inspires and distresses you. Therapists encourage you to question your beliefs about yourself and others. Throughout the session, they maintain eye contact with you, listen actively and push you to recall past events and reflect upon them.

It can be unnerving. It isn't easy to face one's demons, especially when it feels like we're being scrutinized. But it is necessary to open up and communicate. Because without it, we're expecting other people to read our minds and know what we're feeling all the time.

Therapy helps you to become aware of yourself in the present moment, improved communication skills and increases emotional intelligence.

You gain an understanding of yourself and those close to you. You learn what you need, what's expected of you, how to compromise when necessary, and when not to.

You no longer feel alone. You may even get curious and dive deeper into your relationships or events from your past to find out how they shaped your life.

You become more open to change. You learn to accept your past, recognize it as a learning experience and let it go. Perhaps those who caused you pain are sorry themselves; they may have hurt you unintentionally believing their actions were best at the time. But through therapy you will discover it isn't up to you to analyze others' actions; you can only control yourself and hold yourself responsible for what you do.

As you learn to "listen" attentively and empathetically, you develop appreciation for others in your life, and you discover a sense of belonging.

These are the surprising benefits of therapy. Your success becomes infectious. And later on, when you are healed, you can influence your family and friends' lives positively. They might even be impressed by the new you and seek therapy themselves, wanting to grow and be empowered.

SPECIFIC TYPES OF THERAPY

Therapy can be individualized where you meet a counselor on a one-to-one basis, or with you and another person. It stresses self-improvement through self-awareness and soul-searching and teaches coping strategies so that you may make better choices for yourself.

Cognitive Behavioral Therapy (CBT)

Cognitive Behavioral Therapy (CBT) addresses both an individual's cognitive, or mental, abilities and the behavioral problems that emerge from what's perceived as an unfair life. It is a successful method of treatment for conditions like depression, anxiety disorders, and bipolar disorders.

In this type of therapy, the counselor emphasizes thinking about how you feel and what you do about it. Essentially you learn to talk to yourself and question your negative assumptions about yourself and others.

You also analyze your beliefs about past events and determine if they are in any way relevant to your present situations. Are they helping you now? Or are they keeping you stuck in the past?

Couples Therapy

Couples therapy is a special type of CBT that deals with the intermingled problems of couples. It helps to resolve conflicts and restore trust in the relationship. By forming a healthy attachment, couples therapy also renews intimacy.

Family Therapy

Then, sometimes the whole family faces a crisis. This can happen when one member falls ill or suffers from a mental health condition. While providing support and care, the rest of the family is often at a loss, not knowing how to deal with the mental anguish and stress. They may even unknowingly magnify the suffering of the person who is unwell.

A family therapist addresses relationship problems to improve the connection between the family members, helping them with relevant books, support groups, or inviting in close friends and neighbors.

Life is unpredictable; crises happen not once but many times in life. But not all of us have the mental stamina or skills to deal with adversity that involves our closest relationships.

Overall, talking intimately to another person helped me unravel. Awareness of self did not lead to self-acceptance right away because I was still in denial about having a mental disorder, but eventually it helped bring about an "aha" moment that allowed me understand why I had to endure that traumatic event that caused me so much pain. In doing so, I began to forgive myself for leaving my family and friends, and did away with my people pleasing habits.

I learned to accept that most things in life were beyond my control, which promoted self-compassion and resolved much of my anxiety. But that was years down the road.

Exercise Nine: The Road to Recovery

In your companion journal, or on a separate sheet of paper, write down seven things you are proud of yourself for, seven things you forgive yourself for, and make seven different commitments to yourself.

SELF-DECEPTION

When you snicker, is it me you're laughing at?

When you whisper, is it me you're speaking of?

Are you benefiting from such intimidation,

As I avert my eyes, feign pleasantries and smile, attempting to be confident in spite of my shame.

Does it feel good knowing you caused me pain?

Does my misery bolster your swollen head?

When I hang my own in disgrace, trying to sidestep imagining what took place.

How you walked, what was said, where you dined, what all you did.

Did you consider exercising discretion?

Or was it all too easy for those who seen you to look away, pretending not to see what it is they saw

For this reason I can trust no one

Only when I'm alone do I allow myself to let it out and let go

To avoid pretending, time and time again

And at the end of each day I bow my head and pray,

I pray that God might bless this family, that together we might stay.

That these thoughts and visions might be erased,

I pray for my sanity, and that my efforts won't be in vain.

But deep within my heart I know things could never be the same.

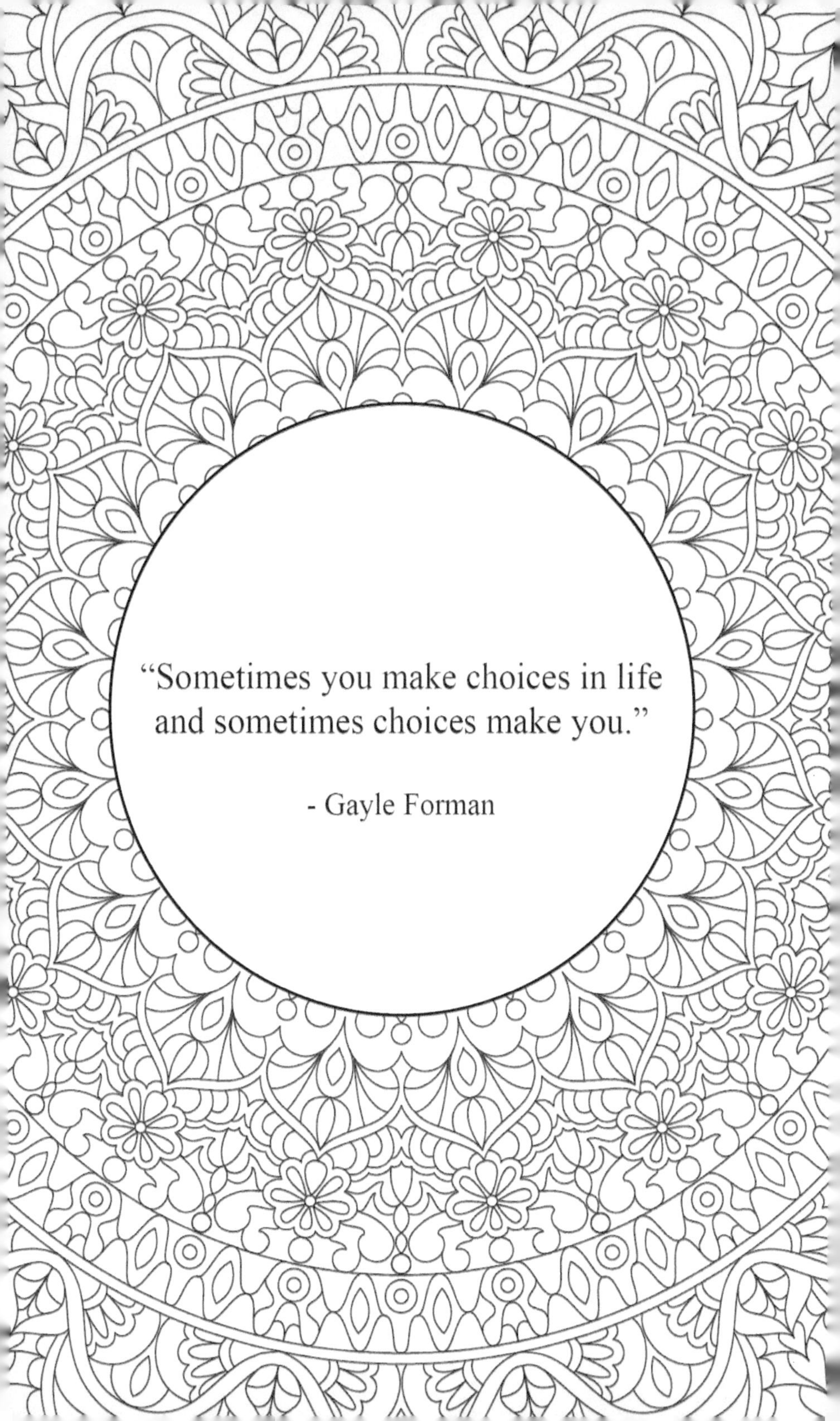

"Sometimes you make choices in life and sometimes choices make you."

- Gayle Forman

Chapter Eight

FOR MY SAKE

DEAR HUSBAND,

As I sit down and write this letter after a therapy session. I want to preface this by saying I'm simply writing my every thought and sharing them in hopes of finally coming to grips with the end of our marriage. This letter does not require a response and if you don't want to reopen old wounds I recommend you delete this email without reading any further.

I have always been torn about the decision to leave. As I've mentioned to you before, I completely shut down and avoided making any decisions while living in the home we once shared. I was the angriest I'd ever been, and still am to this day. And when I did come out of my daze I wanted to hurt you the way you had hurt me. That's how I know what we had was not love. In the past, I've compared it to a parent/child relationship because you were... for the lack of a better word—controlling. It was like when your parents told you not to get up from the table until you finished your veggies. It's possible you meant well. But, as I continued to do what you thought was best, only for things to not play out the way you said they would, disappointment set in.

The difference is, as a child we don't get to choose our parents. The lessons they teach us and the love we have for them are almost an obligation. Although I feel differently towards you now, you were never an obligation. I chose to love you wholeheartedly. I chose to sacrifice for you. I chose to make you my family. So, the anger I felt, and still feel sometimes is disappointing. I love you like family, but I wish to not know you and I don't have that option because we share a child.

I say all that to help you understand where I'm at mentally now. When I moved out I made a list of pros and cons in hopes to figure out the best route for our relationship. It's unfortunate that I'm not capable of forgiveness the way others are. In the past I've stopped talking to my family and had no regrets, so I know that's the easiest thing for me, but that doesn't mean it was right for me to wish I was a single parent.

Your decisions are yours to make and my plan is to one day see you the same way I do my sister. I avoided her for over a year and a half before we established the relationship we have now. And even though she still drives me completely up the wall at times. We fight, we cry, and sometimes we dislike each other, but we find a way to laugh and we move on. Hopefully, I will get there with you. I'm sorry it's taking so long. Today in therapy we discussed why that is. Why I still cry and why it still hurts despite this being my choice. My choices are what led me here. Nevertheless, I wish you well.

Signed,

Your Wife

Even antidepressants and counseling couldn't ease my suffering when I was in the thick of it.

If anything, the antidepressants created a numbness causing me to go about my life, zombie-like, without having any real sense of purpose, and as I mentioned this is truly no way to live.

I knew I was in a toxic relationship, and that I needed to get out of it for my own sake. But I was afraid to translate this awareness into action. It was not just myself I had to consider; I had a son that was only a toddler. I felt my son would blame himself for the separation because that's what I did when my mother and father got divorced.

And I was thoroughly aware of the tremendous aftereffects divorce could have on a child's mind, a sense of loss, anger, and guilt. I knew that he would wonder why mommy and daddy had separate houses or why daddy was not accompanying him to school like all other dads. How would I answer those questions? Do I tell the truth?

I reasoned with myself that it was better to have no relationship than one that was emotionally abusive. My son would eventually understand; I knew from personal experience that children were more than capable of adapting.

But then, I would see him playing with his dad, climbing over his shoulders and experiencing pure joy. His laughter was so infectious that I found myself smiling too. Those were the days I withdrew from making the obvious choice of leaving my husband.

All my childhood fears, insecurities of rejection, and negligence by my parents would haunt me. I would cry myself to sleep. Even then, my painful memories would not disappear; if anything, they were inescapable as they followed me in my dreams.

I was surprised, and grew frustrated, at the intensity. I had no idea my mind could be so destructive. It got to the point that I became incapable of making any decisions and my life seemed to drift into wastefulness.

I would have done just about anything to get rid of the chaos I've come to identify as mental clutter.

WHAT IS MENTAL CLUTTER?

Joseph Ferrari, Ph.D., professor of Community Psychology at the DePaul University, Chicago, once said that mental clutter is a major cause of emotional illness.

Useless and sometimes counterproductive thoughts leave us stuck. These thoughts are often unrelenting as we go on with our chores and responsibilities.

We go to work, read books, watch television, cook, shop, and even celebrate with friends or family, but our thoughts revolve around all the unshakeable negative emotions. Feelings like fear, frustration, loneliness, embarrassment, jealousy, shame, guilt and so much more, follow us around—each with a name, each unhelpful.

Worrying about the future becomes all-consuming we justify it, telling ourselves we can better control our lives if we just make sense of it. But the tendency to worry is dangerous because we think of these situations that haven't happened yet as definite rather than possible outcomes. This type of thinking creates confusion and disorder in our minds.

We hesitate and put off what could free us mentally, emotionally and spiritually. Forcing our present state of distress to take a backseat as we get comfortable with the clutter inside our heads.

MRI scans show that this mental clutter drains reasoning and logical thinking—the result: constant procrastination and decreased efficiency (*Ferrari et al., 2018*). We choose to stay in unhealthy situations, knowing full well how harmful they might be.

We clutter our minds with negative scenarios instead of focusing on other, valid outcomes related to our health or finances. We don't resolve our issues, or even try to get rid of the negative thoughts. We become overwhelmed, and in response our bodies increases the levels of cortisol, as our homes becomes disorganized.

Then we set extremely high expectations and standards for ourselves. Because being a superhuman has been firmly embedded in our minds from childhood, by at least one, if not both of our parents, causing us additional distress and anxiety.

Researchers have further found that women blame themselves for family disturbances more than men. This causes women to feel more disappointed and unsatisfied with their lives. As a result women are nearly twice as likely as men to be diagnosed with depression.

Everything that I went through makes sense in light of this information. It's no wonder that as my marriage dissolved that I became depressed. It was a natural and physical—not just emotional—reaction.

Our assumptions about ourselves, others, and the world deeply affect what we say and how we behave and interpret things. Frequent rejection and painful experiences lead to hurt and a negative self-image. When we hold on to these impractical beliefs, we create mental clutter.

By being kind to ourselves and acknowledging our limitations, we can gradually start getting rid of mental clutter. Dr. Saxby, associate professor of psychology at the University of Southern California in Los Angeles, cautions that clutter is a constant reminder of things that must be done (*Colino, 2022*). He thinks of it as *symbolic pollution* and says that clearing it gives us a sense of pride in a job well done.

Afterwards we feel more capable, confirmed by the greatness of our accomplishments that were once clouded by hurt, rejection, guilt, and worry. These negative emotion are overpowering, and getting rid of them can feel impossible. But once you start, I promise you will feel like you are doing the impossible. And accepting the credit for successfully overcoming them will feel so rewarding!

> "Let us not keep on walking on the broken glass of
>   despair with bleeding words of grief but transcend
>   the viscous discomforts of life and clear out the
>   mountains of clutter in our mind."
>
> — ERIK PEVERNAGIE

HOW TO GET RID OF MENTAL CLUTTER

Our brain processes neurological and emotional data from the various situations we experience. These pieces of information can come from incidents you were involved in, things you've witnessed, or things you heard from television or social media. Which is why it is important to make time to declutter your mind on a regular basis.

Clearing emotional clutter helps you to notice the feelings you've kept hidden or avoided. Because you're finally recognizing them and processing your emotions, you develop more awareness and clarity of your thoughts. It's an alleviating aftereffect that brings compassion and joy, knowing you can trust yourself to take care of yourself. Once this happens, it's easier for you to forgive yourself and others and open yourself to embrace the world with unconditional love.

Unburden Yourself

Take a moment to release your emotions. I once did it while meditating on the beach, as the waves of the ocean crashed into the sand underneath me creating a sort of healing pulse and serene softness. I placed my hands in the sand, and closed my eyes, trying to soak up the ambience. I felt immensely safe and grounded. I poured my heart out on that beach and pleaded with God to help me survive and keep me safe. Afterwards I felt unburdened.

You can unburden your feelings in a journal. Practice stream of consciousness writing by jotting down everything that comes to your mind. Don't worry about complete sentences or punctation, simply express your worries, griefs, anger, and hurt as it pops into your mind.

By consistently emptying your emotions into a journal, you will find relief. You will gradually develop a new outlook on life, and be able to guide your thoughts and emotions in the right direction.

Quiet your Mind

Close your eyes, concentrate your mind on the spot between your eyebrows and empty your mind of thoughts. At first, you may find it impossible to stop your mind from babbling. You'll find yourself distracted, pulling your attention to hundreds of unimportant things that drain your level of productivity.

You'll need to meditate to stop your mind from going into the past or trying to predict the future. The easiest way to meditate is to focus your attention on your breathing. As you slowly breathe in and out, occasionally taking deep breaths, appreciate how your body begins to relax.

Identify Opportunities to Grow

All of your memories and the feelings you have about them are not accurate. We tend to focus on negative events and situations and ignore the good memories and times. It is how we develop a victim mindset that plays against our better interests.

To have a growth mindset and be in an empowering position, try to recall the memories that put a smile on your face or times you've prevailed in difficult situations.

Acknowledge that there are memories that are not so happy. But, instead of feeling bad about them, use them as an opportunity to find enlightenment and grow. What did you learn from those experiences? Allow those memories to motivate and strengthen you, and know that our experiences themselves are not good or bad; our interpretation is what defines them.

Implement Healthy Boundaries

Before you start doing something, ask yourself whether you will be happy doing it if you got nothing in return. If your answer is no, take that as a cue to evaluate if this is something you really must do, and if so set some boundaries and limitations.

"Let It Go"

I came across a quote by John Mark Green that said, *"As you remove toxic people from your life, you free up space and emotional energy for positive, healthy relationships."* When relationships have turned out to be toxic and are emotionally exhausting, it's time to say goodbye; that season has ended.

If the relationship is the kind that you can't get rid of–if a family member or one of your coworkers is toxic, for example–then put them in a position (in your mind if you're unable to do so physically) where they no longer affect your mental and emotional health.

PROCESSING EMOTIONS AND FEELINGS

Have you ever taken the time to question if your emotions were valid? Whether you should be feeling a way at all? If you haven't you should.

Evolutionary biologists and psychologists believe that emotions like worry, grief, sadness, shame, anger, etc., have progressive backgrounds. They represent the dominant force by which social groups function (Wilson & Wilson, 2007).

They are a response to social behaviors, and in turn, they instigate us to behave in certain ways (*Nesse, 2019*).

As emotions have evolved within social frameworks, we can regulate them, either by ourselves or with the help of social group members (*Nesse, 2019*). There are components established within the social group that help make emotional healing possible. These include emotional contagion, empathy, perspective-taking, and mentalization by group members to internalize the distress of another belonging to the same social group (*de Waal & Preston, 2017*).

Exercise Ten: Clarifying the Chaos

In your companion journal or on a separate sheet of paper, make a list of things you consider essential to your life. Do this to clear out the clutter in your life and try to adapt to a minimalist lifestyle.

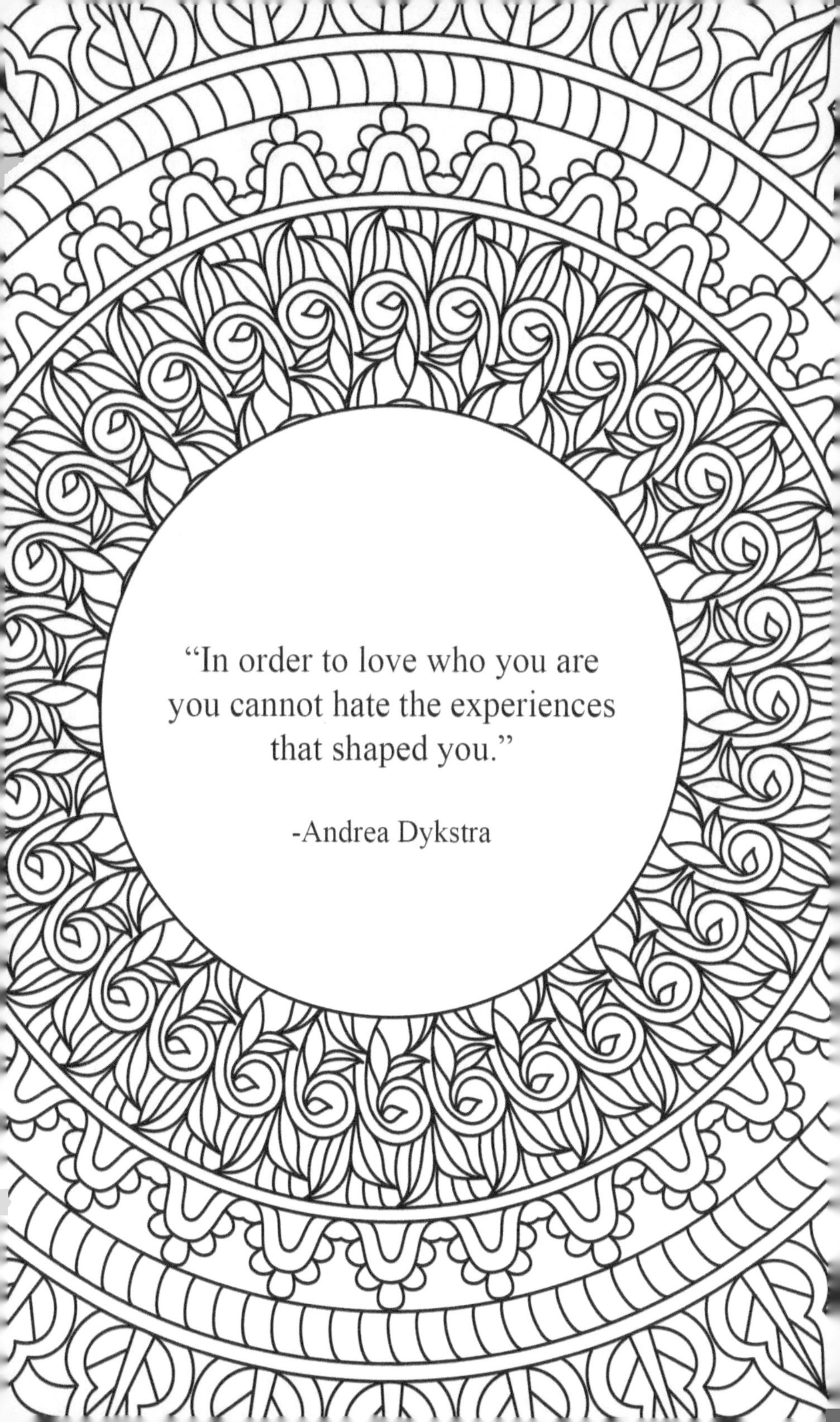
"In order to love who you are
you cannot hate the experiences
that shaped you."

-Andrea Dykstra

Chapter Nine

THE JOURNEY TO SELF-HEALING

STAGES OF EMOTIONAL HEALING

NOBODY WANTS TO SUFFER. Suffering shatters our core development. Our first response to depression is often disbelief and denial. These emotions leads to all kinds of toxic emotions, therefore psychologists advise you to work *through* your pain and understand that it is a part of life and not something you can escape. Use it as an experience to help you progress, and grow stronger mentally and emotionally.

Here are the various stages you go through when you're healing.

Sitting in Discomfort

With good reason, you may not be ready to address the cause of your unhappiness. You may know what's troubling you, and even have a medical diagnosis, but still not be ready to face it just yet. Instead, you prefer to run away from it all. But don't give in to the urge to hide. Acknowledging the pain and identifying your triggers will help you be honest with yourself about your feelings.

Naming Your Feelings

It will help you to label what you're feeling. Identifying your emotions by name: helpless, frustrated, guilty, skeptical, weak, jealous, embarrassed, etc. Naming them identifies the wounds that you need to heal. Use the feeling wheel previously provided if necessary.

Truthful Expression

Once you've identified and named your emotions—*feel them*! Cry if you are sad, shout and scream if you are enraged, and allow the negative energy the opportunity to leave your body.

Society has conditioned us—once again!—this time to believe that negative feelings shouldn't be on display. Phrases like "cool as a cucumber" are used to indicate that we should be unemotional during distressing times, and "stay strong" by holding them in. Children are told by adults "don't be sad" and "don't cry" and even—in some cases—"I'll give you something to cry about!", meaning that a child should just "suck it up" and "deal". So even in childhood, we are taught to ignore and suppress our emotions.

However, doing this is destructive to the body and mind, causing illnesses like high blood pressure and heart attacks, and feelings of inferiority and bewilderment. These destructive emotions cause mental lethargy and withdrawal, and when suppressed for long periods of time, they erupt like a volcano causing tragic results.

When you allow yourself to express your emotions, you gradually come to terms with them. You learn that you are not alone in your grief, and find reasons to be happy again.

Acceptance and Self-Awareness

Once you accept your feelings, they no longer make you feel hopeless. You accept the limitations of others' that are making you feel the way you do.

You know who and what triggers your trauma, and can face them without losing yourself in the process. Every time you succeed, you feel accomplished and gain strength from knowing you can accomplish anything you put your mind to.

You are now more prepared to understand others' perspectives and sympathize with them. You can show love and trust. You create authentic connections with others and best of all, you come to learn your purpose in life.

Once you begin to heal emotionally, you'll find that you are calmer, and won't feel like used or disappointed by other people all the time. You embrace your past experiences and look at them more logically, with curiosity and compassion instead of sadness and bitterness.

You will enjoy your present life and find yourself complaining less. You are open to learn new skills and eager to make positive and meaningful contributions in life.

You take care of your health and develop routines. You sleeping better at night. All the physical pain—aches in your muscles and joints, soreness, and migraines are gone. Your appetite returns. You feel rejuvenated and grounded.

This is the stage when you will feel that you don't need your psychiatric medication anymore and can take steps in discontinuing your use of them to stay focused on your present life.

Your scars symbolize a battle you fought and won. They motivate you to help others who remind you of your old self. This is where I am, and this is my goal for you.

I was a damaged individual with extremely low self-esteem and self-confidence. I believed that I was unworthy of unconditional love. Nothing lasted in my life. My parents got divorced, and I was dragged to a new place and had to accommodate a new way of life without guidance. My mother and father rejected me when I needed them the most. They thought more about their life and wanted me to fit in. But that is not how it should work.

I was trying to be like someone I wasn't, and studied for grades without really being interested in education. At the time, however, I still felt that wasn't enough, and strived to cultivate an image that would portray how accomplished I was. I was into so many conflicting and contradictory things that I lost track of what I was doing and why? An intense desire to show people how perfect I was, egged me on. I was on a mission to be loved and validated. Without outside validation, my whole life meant nothing.

I fell in love with a man who I thought was interesting and handsome. I didn't give myself enough time to understand what I was really looking for in a romantic relationship. To me, a whirlwind affair meant an escape from the reality of existence. Little did I know, I was moving from a bad situation to one that was worse.

I was looking for love and didn't even love myself. How could others appreciate me when I desperately needed them to reassure me and cater to my feelings all the time? I learned through pain and experience that we should take care of ourselves, look deep within to get to the bottom of past miseries and resolve them with forgiveness and kindness.

I was fortunate to find a therapist who taught me the value of self-love and self-compassion.

Pain teaches us life's greatest lessons that we would never have learned otherwise: the necessity of finding the meaning of pain. It changes our attitude and thoughts towards ourselves and others. The significance of emotional pain and trauma overwhelms us with mistrust, irritation, and cynicism. Each of these emotions is damaging enough to evoke hordes of memories of all the times we felt unwanted, insecure, and unloved, and questioned the validity of our feelings. We feel as if those in our immediate circles can't help us because they aren't in our shoes to understand what we're going through. We feel violated and cheated as if our whole life is coming apart.

And we may recover from our sad emotional state, but recovery does not mean we are healed. We are still heartbroken, holding deep irreconcilable grudges against those who harmed or hurt us, and the brunt of our assault is directed toward ourselves and our loved ones. We snap at the slightest annoyance striking back defensively, rarely thinking about the aftereffects or consequences. We suffer from a different kind of anxiety and distress, withdrawing from others, believing we no longer want love.

But this isn't healing. Emotional wounds also need closure like any other type of wound. This is why we talk so much about moving on or forgiving people. We must take better care of ourselves, determine what we really need–before we can open up to consider a relationship with anyone else. Like they say during flights, "Should an emergency situation occur, secure your own oxygen mask first before assisting others."

We must learn to live in peace, submit to our feelings to acknowledge and validate ourselves, and allow harmony and happiness to settle in. That, according to Oprah Winfrey, is living in wisdom.

We must remember no matter what that other people will not change unless they find it necessary. But, if nothing changes, nothing changes. Therefore, we ourselves must change in order to evolve because every day of the month and every month of the years that roll by the pain is slowly killing us.

Self-healing is about deliverance, respectability, and freedom from past mistakes and the people that are holding us back. It's about knowing for sure that there are other and more healthy options to express our emotions instead of sabotaging ourselves all the time. And isn't that something we all wish for ourselves?

Exercise Eleven: Taking a Hard Look at Self

In your companion journal or on a separate sheet of paper write five positive attributes people may have commended you on or some of your favorite compliments. These could have come from anyone, and be about anything. (Your looks, your style, your work ethic, anything.) Do you believe these to be right/true? Why or why not?

Now, write down five pieces of constructive criticism, or feedback, you've been given that's affected you long-term. Do you believe these to be right/true? Why or why not?

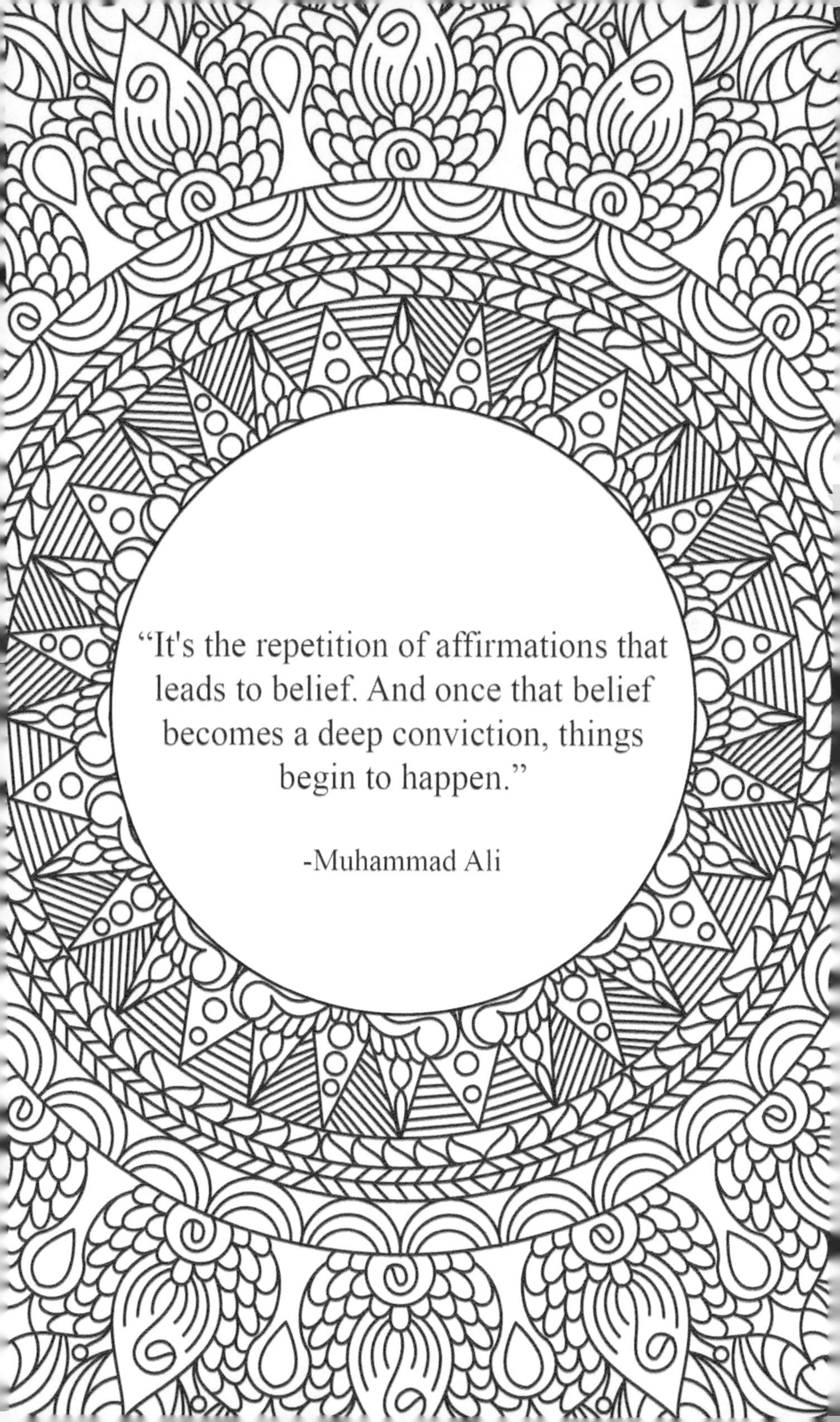

"It's the repetition of affirmations that leads to belief. And once that belief becomes a deep conviction, things begin to happen."

-Muhammad Ali

Chapter Ten

ALTERNATIVE THERAPY

THE POWER OF POSITIVE AFFIRMATIONS

POSITIVE AFFIRMATIONS ARE expressions that *affirm* something to be true. They are sentences that we repeat to ourselves to stop ourselves from thinking and believing negative thoughts. These thoughts surface from time to time, sometimes without apparent reasons and at other times triggered by people, situations or events. To repel our fears, occasionally unwarranted, we must say something soothing and positive to ourselves.

Sometimes we are victims of what is known as a *self-fulfilling prophecy*. All this means is that what we believe to be true will become true. For example, if you're told as a child that you are bad, after a while, you will come to believe that to be true—whether it is, or not. And as a result, you behave badly. Why should you try to be otherwise? You no longer care because all you've been told is that you are bad anyway and that negative feedback has become your truth.

On the other hand, if we're told positive things about ourselves and believe them, those "prophecies" are also self-fulfilling.

Isn't it much better to think positively and encourage positive beliefs in our thoughts versus negative ones?

Positive affirmations are proven to work in psychological practice. It is simple. It means choosing a phrase and going over it in our minds or out loud repeatedly. It requires consistent practice for at least 10 minutes every day to make permanent changes in our way of thinking.

Additionally, mirror therapy is a useful tool for emotional distress. Let us find out how it works.

WHAT IS MIRROR THERAPY?

In mirror therapy, conflict resolution occurs by tricking—or retraining—the brain. Our brain is the compelling organ, processing environmental information through the five senses. But the strongest of our senses is vision, because as humans we tend to rely on our sight more than anything else.

That's the reason mirror therapy was used to heal the "phantom pain" of people who had lost their limbs following amputation.

It's a fact that amputees frequently experience pain and unpleasant sensations—like itching—which feels as if it's in the limb no longer attached to their bodies. This happens because of the interrupted communication between the brain and the affected limb. The brain sends commands to the limb to carry out certain functions and these—of course—get held up on the way.

As a result, patients sought relief from their mental conflict and misery, and scientists devised mirror therapy to trick the brain into believing that the amputated limb still existed and functioned.

In the original experiment, the individual looked at his affected limb in a mirror while moving his normal limb and imagined the movement in the amputated limb. After three weeks of training, more than half of the participants "felt" some degree of activity in the affected limb, and their aching and uncomfortableness decreased.

Doctors used vision to fool the brain that its information was reaching the intended place, in this case, the amputated limb.

HOW DOES IT HAPPEN?

It's said that the brain has *mirror neurons*, nerve fibers that are stimulated when you are doing something, but also when you see others doing something. These actions must be things you can actually do. Therefore, mirror neurons aren't activated when a bird drops mid-flight because you can't fly.

These neurons are also activated when you imagine an action being done without having to actually do it. This function of the brain is utilized in mirror therapy (*Faure & others, 2019*).

Researchers at the Rockefellers University, New York, found that cells continued cell renewal in the brain's hippocampus region regardless of age or time. This region is responsible for learning, memory, and emotions. Which means we can re-educate our brains to learn new skills.

The brain can consistently learn to process information better by making or removing specific synaptic pathways, or brain waves, that seem to fit the conditions.

Overall, our efforts are towards conflict resolution. We can do that either consciously or automatically.

MIRROR THERAPY IN COGNITIVE BEHAVIORAL PROBLEMS

Mirror therapy, as a form of alternative therapy, can help in various ways, one of which is body image. Since this is a dominant problem in many women, and something I experienced firsthand, I will discuss it.

I was once friends with a girl who had an eating disorder. Her counselor told her that she maintained a particular image or size in her mind that she considered her "ideal body." If she could make her body look like the image in her mind, she thought her eating disorder problem would be cured.

Taylor grew up with Barbie dolls and fairy tales. Her concept of a woman's body was influenced by supermodels like Cindy Crawford and Naomi Campbell. She knew that each of us came with a particular body type; we couldn't change our heights, the girth of our limbs, or body proportions.

Despite this, Taylor longed for a body that wasn't possible for her frame or her genetics. She obsessed over the state of her figure, working out to the point of punishment and engaging in alternative cycles of binging, vomiting, and fasting.

This is surprisingly common; negative self-esteem has been linked with eating disorder problems or body dysmorphic disorder (when a victim is engrossed with a particular part of their body, like the size of their hips or thighs, or breasts). Unlike women with a healthy outlook on their bodies, victims with body dysmorphic disorder look at the mirror, scanning and amplifying what they consider a defect of their bodies. They just can't see that they are already beautiful, or that they've become skin-and-bones. All they see is the image of themselves they've created in their minds; a feeling of self-rejection or disgust overwhelms their minds. This negative opinion also hurts people who they are in a relationship with them because who wants to watch their loved one suffer in such a way?

As with all sufferers of body dysmorphia, Taylor's health dangerously deteriorated. Fortunately, however, she learned about mirror therapy and was able to recover from her low self-confidence.

In the journal *Clinical Psychological Review*, an article published by Griffen and colleagues suggested that mirror therapy is beneficial for these patients. In the sessions in which therapists of the same gender assists the patient, the patient gets into a sexy outfit and looks at themselves in the mirror.

It works one of three ways:

- **Guided Non-Judgmental Mirror Exposure Therapy** - In the first method, the individual stands before a full-length three-way mirror and concentrates on their body. They start from their hair and move gradually down, taking the same amount of time to describe each of their body parts objectively, using neutral language as if they were trying to assist someone in sketching their pictures.

- **Pure Mirror Exposure Therapy** - In this method, the participant narrates their emotions while describing their body.

- **Mirror Exposure With a Positive Focus** - Those who can't tolerate looking at their body objectively use this method. The individual has to comment positively on the lovable parts of their body and say, "I have such a beautiful neck," or "My complexion is really fair."

HOW DOES MIRROR THERAPY HELP?

Mirror therapy helps modify one's interpretation of a situation, or other concerns related to cognitive dysfunction. Instead of thinking that your friends don't invite you because you are boring, you will think, "My friends didn't ask me this time probably because it was a closed group meeting about something that doesn't concern me. I will call them later and find out."

Your attitude becomes more unbiased and nonchalant. It reduces stress and upholds relationships.

You stop paying attention to counterproductive and undesirable thoughts because you don't look at an imperfect world through the scope of prejudice. Instead, you open up to consider a bigger picture and look at things from a broader perspective.

In another variety of mirror therapy, called exposure therapy, an individual who is terrified of something is encouraged to face their fears and question them. Continual exposure to the fears reduces their intensity.

Mirror therapy also aids in resolving cognitive dissonance. It is a method that challenges your assumptions about a problem. The more you focus on the contradicting possibility, the easier for you accept to it as truth.

For example, your friend is learning French. She encourages you to accompany her. You keep denying your friend because you don't want to humiliate yourself. You think you could never learn a new language.

But if you keep contradicting your belief, a time will come when you agree that you *can* learn French if you try.

Exercise Twelve: Looking Back to Move Forward

In your companion journal or on a separate sheet of paper, write down two significant events you have tried to forget. Then write down how you overcame them.

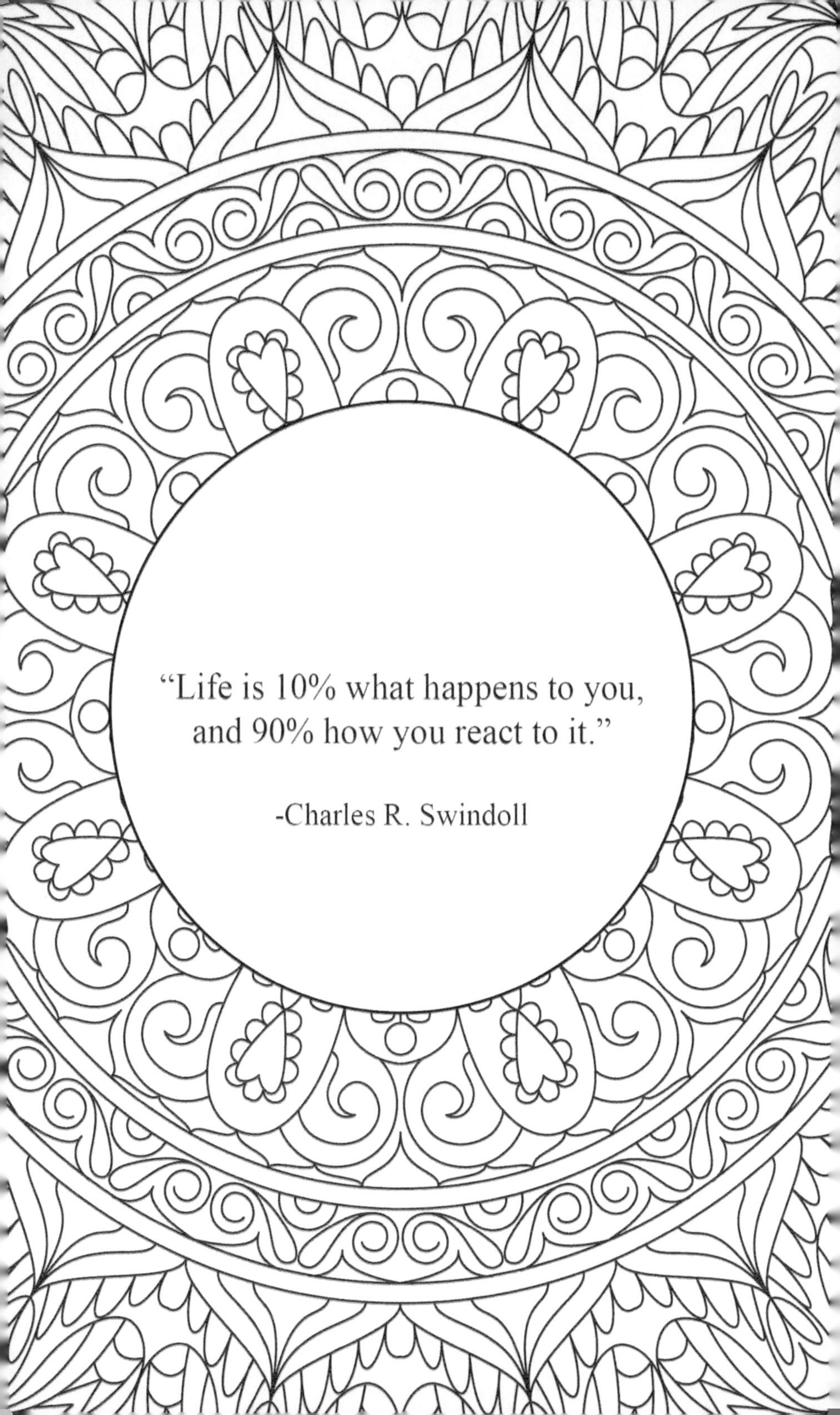
"Life is 10% what happens to you,
and 90% how you react to it."

-Charles R. Swindoll

Chapter Eleven

HEALTH LIES IN LIVING

THE WORLD HEALTH ORGANIZATION defines health as a state of physical, mental, and social well-being. But this definition was established back in 1947.

More recently, the green paper, *Our Healthier Nation*, laid greater importance on the emotional health of an individual. Health, accordingly, has been considered as *"being confident and positive and able to cope with ups and downs of life (Stewart-Brown et al., 1998)."*

It is proved by scientific research that emotional torment can cause an individual to suffer from physical illnesses. Chronic stress modifies the immune system by suppressing it. It raises the chances of viral infections and is linked to various other illnesses like asthma, diabetes, and high blood pressure.

When we are emotionally distressed, we often disregard self-care routines. Smoking, drinking, and eating fast foods loaded with fats, sugars, and salt are common avenues for how we release emotional stress ultimately changing the acidity of the stomach. Which can lead to stress ulcers.

Merriam-Webster defines wellness as *"the quality or state of being in good health, especially as an actively sought goal."*

As I see it, wellness is a balance of body and mind. It encompasses physical, emotional, spiritual, social, environmental, and financial wellness.

We are healthy when all aspects of our lives are in harmony. Physical illnesses can be diagnosed and treated and emotional turmoil is nearly nonexistent. Naturally, emotional health becomes more important in this context.

We often equate emotional health with mental health. But, emotional health deals with the "feelings" that you have as your mind processes the information it gathers every day. According to Julie Fraga, PsyD, emotional health means you are in harmony with your feelings, strengths, and weaknesses.

It means that you are aware of your feelings. You accept these feelings for what they are. But, you try to cope with the emotions instead of being overwhelmed by them or denying their existence. You take time to process your emotions, considering how best to express them without hurting yourself or others in the process (*Jennison, 2020*).

Bettering your emotional health does not mean that you will never feel bad, angry, sad, or hurt. You still have your ups and downs, which correlate with your environment and circumstances.

Personally, I'm still using the feelings wheel, writing a lot of emotions, and crying in private. But, the goal is to try to be rational about what you're feeling instead of being in a defensive, annoyed. Otherwise you will lose confidence in your capabilities regarding coping with different situations: some good, some bad, and others ugly, exposing your mind and body to mental stress.

Emotional health is not the same for everyone. Some of us can process information more quickly. We sense ourselves being triggered but do not get worked up. We make peace with our feelings and adapt to our circumstances in everyday living.

When we learn to take care of our emotional health, we are more receptive to other people in our lives. We don't get irritated or frustrated by the highs and lows of normal social interactions.

But, why is it important to maintain our emotional health daily? If you think about it, you will find that emotional health makes you more resilient; you have courage, possess wherewithal and determination, plus you will build more meaningful relationships.

Empathy and compassion for yourself make your relationships more stable. You can perceive what others feel and need and your relationships endure despite hardships.

Your self-esteem is enhanced, your thought processes are clearer, and your thoughts, emotions, and actions are in alignment with your positive mental state. They portray how you are feeling about yourself inside and out, improving your immunity and physical energy.

HOW TO IMPROVE EMOTIONAL HEALTH

Improving your emotional health is an ongoing process. You need to practice being accountable for your feelings all the time.

Fraga mentioned that you must be aware of your feelings. As you previously mentioned naming them can help is extremely important. Do this calmly and avoid getting distracted by negative self-talk.

Transform your self-criticisms to self-love and compassion. By doing so you are mindful of the image you are presenting to the world.

But this does not mean you should question or repress your feelings. You are simply changing your *reactions* to emotions.

PRACTICING EMOTIONAL REGULATION

As stated, emotional regulation is an active process. You can execute this by meditation, journaling, music, or, if necessary—getting professional help.

Mindful Meditation

During meditation you tune out your immediate environment. You focus on what you are feeling and sensing at the moment without judgment. For instance, if you have pain from sitting in a cross-legged position, recognize the pain without believing that it's bad to sit cross-legged or that your knees are getting weak.

Mindful meditation involves breathing techniques, guided imagery, and other relaxation methods. It is the best choice to decompress after a stressful day. It guides your attention away from negative or disorganized thoughts that distract your attention and drain your energy. This form of meditation relieves stress, anxiety, pain, insomnia, and high blood pressure.

While in practice focus on feelings of love, gratitude, joy, excitement, hope, satisfaction, and prosperity. And avoiding feelings of doubt or disappointment, boredom, arrogance, fear, resentment, hate, revenge, anger, criticism, or worry. Learn to pay attention to the traditional senses (hearing sight, smell, taste, and touch), you've been utilizing absent-mindedly. Doing so will steadily make you aware of how powerful and in control of yourself you are.

Practice mindful meditation either in a sitting posture in a quiet place or walking and concentrating on your movements and sensations of posture. Both are equally as effective.

Journaling

Journaling your thoughts and emotions must be done regularly to receive true benefit from it. Write how you genuinely feel about your day in a simple manner. To make it easy, you can even journal your thoughts in a note on your cell phone.

Let the words pour from your heart without filtering them. You can also doodle or draw pictures if you express your emotions better that way.

Keeping a journal helps you to face your worries, anxieties, and fears; while also recording your accomplishments and memorable moments. As you document them regularly, you will find yourself solving negative thought patterns and resolving conflict more easily.

Therapeutic Music

Music can be uplifting, restoring the body and mind. But more importantly, binaural music can help decrease blood pressure, elevate your mood by improving concentration, relax your mind, and divert your attention from negative emotions. You feel more connected to your feelings through music. And the right frequency of music can even aid in providing you with a good night's sleep.

Practicing Gratitude

One of the reasons for our misfortune is we are eager to satisfy our wants, desires, and cravings. While engaging in superficial or impulsive activities, we tend to forget the good things we already have in our lives. Denying they exist unintentionally makes us feel worse. We chase things that don't truly matter. In the process, sacrificing our comfort and well-being.

Practicing gratitude before you go to bed by saying a prayer, or *feeling* appreciative, makes you realize how blessed your life truly is regardless of our circumstances.

PAYING ATTENTION TO YOUR HEALTH

Good physical health is like currency. We earn it through self-discipline and self-care. Therefore you should eat nutritious food, get enough sleep and exercise. You should avoid smoking and consume alcohol in moderation. Once in a while, "cheat days" are acceptable, but as you practice discipline and self-regulation, you will discover that you can enjoy healthy options even on your cheat days.

Food

Food nourishes the body and mind.

Eating raw fruits, fresh vegetables, and whole-grain cereals helps us live longer. These types of foods are natural sources of vitamins, fibers, and antioxidants. They lower bad cholesterol and keep our hearts and gut healthy. They are truly superfoods.

Your diet which should include three main meals and two snacks a day should contain enough foods that are beneficial to your health. And you should also drink plenty of water to keep your body hydrated.

Exercise

Exercise releases potent chemicals called endorphins. They act like morphine in reducing pain sensations and elevating our mood. They produce a condition described as "runner's high." That's why exercise reduces anxiety and depression and also helps you sleep well.

But there are many other benefits of exercise. You improve muscle and bone strength. Your posture and balance are preserved, and the effects are more distinct in postmenopausal women.

Exercise also reduces blood sugar and blood pressure. Plus, if you exercise outdoors, you get the benefits of receiving vitamin D from the sun.

Exercise at least thirty minutes a day, any time of the day. Aerobic exercises like swimming, running, jogging, cycling, and speed walking are the best choices. It should be combined with stretching and toning exercises. You can also break up your exercise routine into ten-minute increments if you are unable to exercise for longer periods of time.

Sleep

According to the Centers for Disease Control and Prevention (CDC), we should sleep at least seven to eight hours a day. Reduced sleep duration has been linked to asthma, depression, and heart attack.

Good sleep is healing. It removes the toxins accumulating in the brain.

Without proper sleep, you can easily become nervous and emotionally unstable. Studies have shown this can cause repetitive negative thoughts that affect your day-to-day performance, outlook on life, and relationships.

STRENGTHEN YOUR SOCIAL RELATIONSHIPS

No one can deny that our happiest moments are those we spend with the people closest to us. They can be our parents, children, partners, or like-minded friends. The more we share time with them, the better we adjust to life.

Forming meaningful connections with others is integral to human life. It extends from your family to your immediate neighborhood and into the community.

With the advancement of social media, connection has developed new meaning. Despite the convenience of social media and the internet, nothing makes us happier than real-life human contact, especially when it's meaningful and supportive. However, we must beware of those that appear friendly but are hostile, narcissists, and toxic individuals.

Exercise Thirteen: Filling the Void

In your companion journal, or on a separate sheet of paper, ask yourself, what do I love about life? If nothing immediately comes to mind, write down 25 things that bring you joy and/or things you want to focus on in the future.

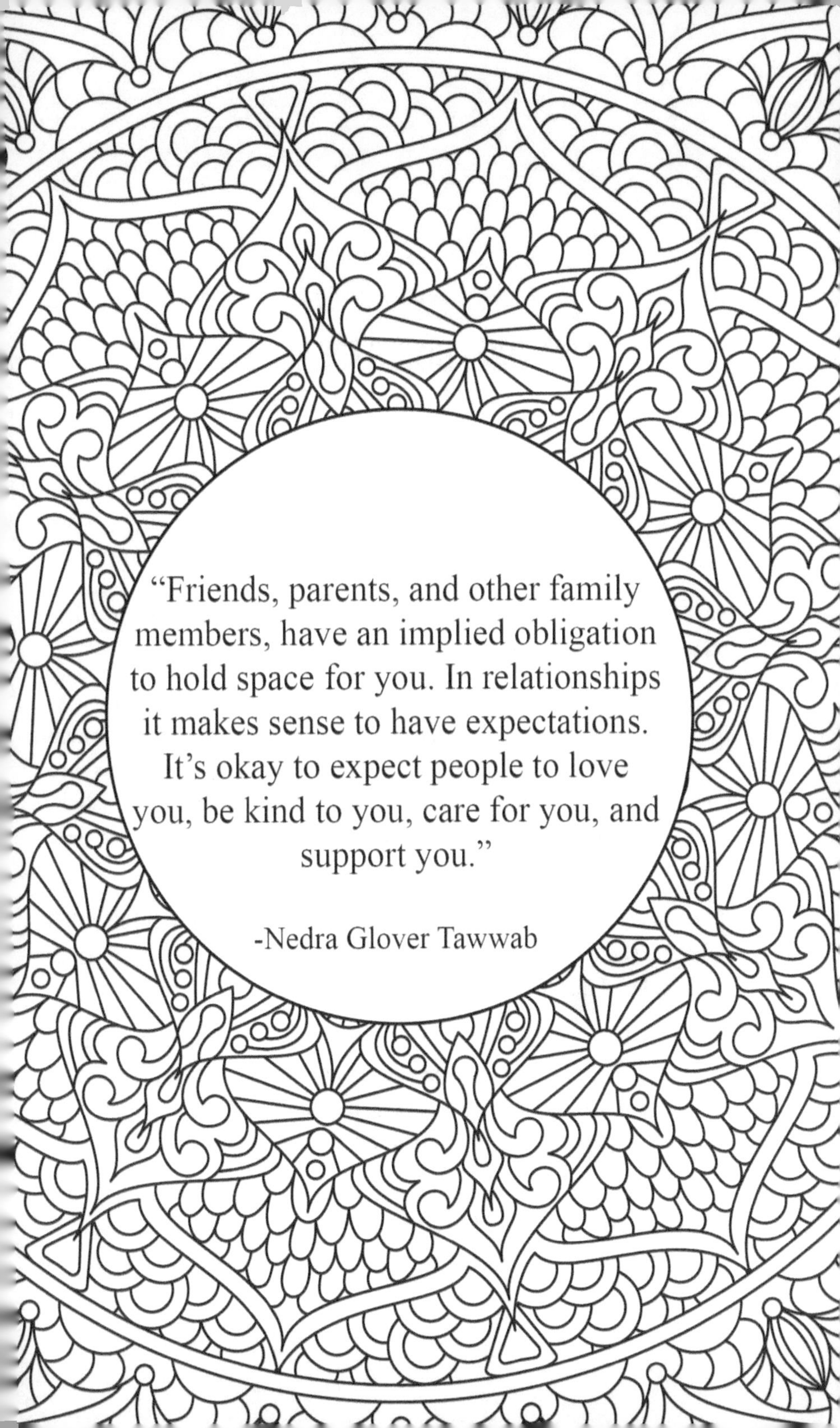

"Friends, parents, and other family members, have an implied obligation to hold space for you. In relationships it makes sense to have expectations. It's okay to expect people to love you, be kind to you, care for you, and support you."

-Nedra Glover Tawwab

Chapter Twelve

SOMETIMES LOSSES ARE NECESSARY

WHAT IS A *TOXIC* PERSON? We have often heard about toxic relationships, but what makes someone truly toxic?

They are usually the people who are dealing with a lot of negativity in their lives. You may find that you're uncomfortable around them for some reason. They pour their hopeless energy and emotions into you, stressing you out. They manipulate your feelings, or gaslight you; making you feel bad about yourself. You find yourself constantly explaining yourself.

They harbor tons of negativity and hurt, buried deep within, which changes their outlook on life. Leaving them feeling discouraged, skeptical and distrustful.

All of us have some degree of negative bias which means negative thoughts, feelings, and circumstances can sometimes influence our emotions more than the good things happening to us. However, only pessimistic people allow their negative bias to control their lives.

Our upbringing can shape how we focus on life's events. However, negativity has also been linked to genetic or environmental causes. Therefore, some of us by nature are anxious or the worrying kind.

When parents often complain and point out the negative things in life, their children unconsciously become experts in focusing on the negatives of life more than the positives. They learn to talk, behave and think in a way that discourages people who are in contact with them.

Toxic people do not like to see others happy or have peace of mind. Imagine, crabs in a barrel; they pull each other down, because "if I can't have it, neither can you." Such personalities prevent others from realizing their full potential because they are devoted to presenting negative pictures of a situation versus positive.

If you have someone like this in your life, get rid of them; trust me, you're better off without them. During my journey of becoming self-actualized I ended one of my longest friendships, after several attempts to "work it out". It wasn't until I cut her off that I realized that ending unhealthy friendships was also a sign of growth.

YOU ARE WHO YOU HANG WITH

Consider how you are when you are with toxic people. Do you eventually find yourself thinking negatively too? Before you answer me, let's examine a few common negative thought processes.

Catastrophizing

Negative-minded personalities make mountains out of molehills. They awfulize or catastrophize every event or situation: regarding everything as bad. For instance, if you want to travel somewhere new, they will tell you not to because you may have an accident, or will bring up how dangerous it is.

Minimization

If they exaggerate the bad things, they will often minimize the good things. Causing them to be real Debbie Downers.

All or Nothing

Furthermore, those that think negatively will see things as either good or bad, there is no in between. This kind of mentality is borderline judgmental and ignores hundreds of other possibilities in life. Because as I mentioned, even a bad situation is not all bad. If you think about it, you should always be able to find a silver lining.

Overgeneralization

They assume that if a situation turns out negatively for them, all future situations will produce the same results.

Negative Attention

The attention of negative-minded people is on bad things that happen to them. They seem to forget the good things that also happen in their lives.

By associating with people that think this way, you will begin to think this way also. You will start to feel unsettled and drained because it takes a heavy toll on your mind to process such pessimism. Oftentimes codependent, these individuals start to plant fear and doubts in your mind with their "concerns", and want to be a part of all your plans. Forcing you to be empathetic towards their emotions and always be there for them.

Negative-minded people do not think of your success, which has no meaning to them. All they worry about is being "left behind." They are at their manipulative best when they are projecting their insecurities on others. They constantly ignore boundaries, triggering powerful emotions and conflicts, disregarding your personal space.

They deplete your spirit and energy like leeches, erasing the core of who you are, leaving you with feelings of hopelessness, making healthy living impossible.

This is why it is important to choose your friends carefully and get rid of those who have a crab mentality. And don't worry about getting rid of the toxic people in your life. They are the ones who want a shoulder to cry on. But when you need them, they aren't there for you.

If someone in your life is overly cynical and sees the worse in everything and almost everybody, you are connecting with the wrong person. Negativity is contagious and leads to self-doubt. You avoid taking calculated risks fearing failures and rejections. You lose faith in the system and other people.

Yet to reach your goal, you will need to trust the right kind of people. Healthy friendships have respect for personal boundaries; they allow each person in the relationship to thrive.

They're the ones who will encourage you to take healthy risks and support you thereafter, which will bring you greater rewards in the future. This can be about your health, career, education, family, and relationships.

Friendships should be empowering, not diminishing, and always have your best interest in mind. Allowing you to feel confident and in control of your life.

And if they are like-minded people with similar interests they will not think of you as competition, they will share your joys, concerns, and dreams for the future. They will be true friends who will hold you accountable and do what is required to push you to go further in life.

Exercise Fourteen: Building Life-Changing Friendships

In your companion journal, or on a separate sheet of paper, write down the characteristics you like most about your closest friend and/or confidant, and also the things you don't like. What personality traits will you look for in other people that you could build a healthy, long-lasting friendship with?

ALTER EGO

Support me, don't judge me
Encourage me and enlighten me
In fragile circumstances it's important you handle me with care
Consider my feelings, all of them
Don't embarrass me or pressure me
Walk with me, not always literally but figuratively
Have faith and stand beside me,
Some might call this loyalty
Don't doubt me, trust in me
Really listen and engage with me
Show interest in our conversations; actively listen to me
Be flexible and compromising
I sometimes require a lot of patience
And if there's a change in me, don't abandon me
These are the times I'll need you to be there for me

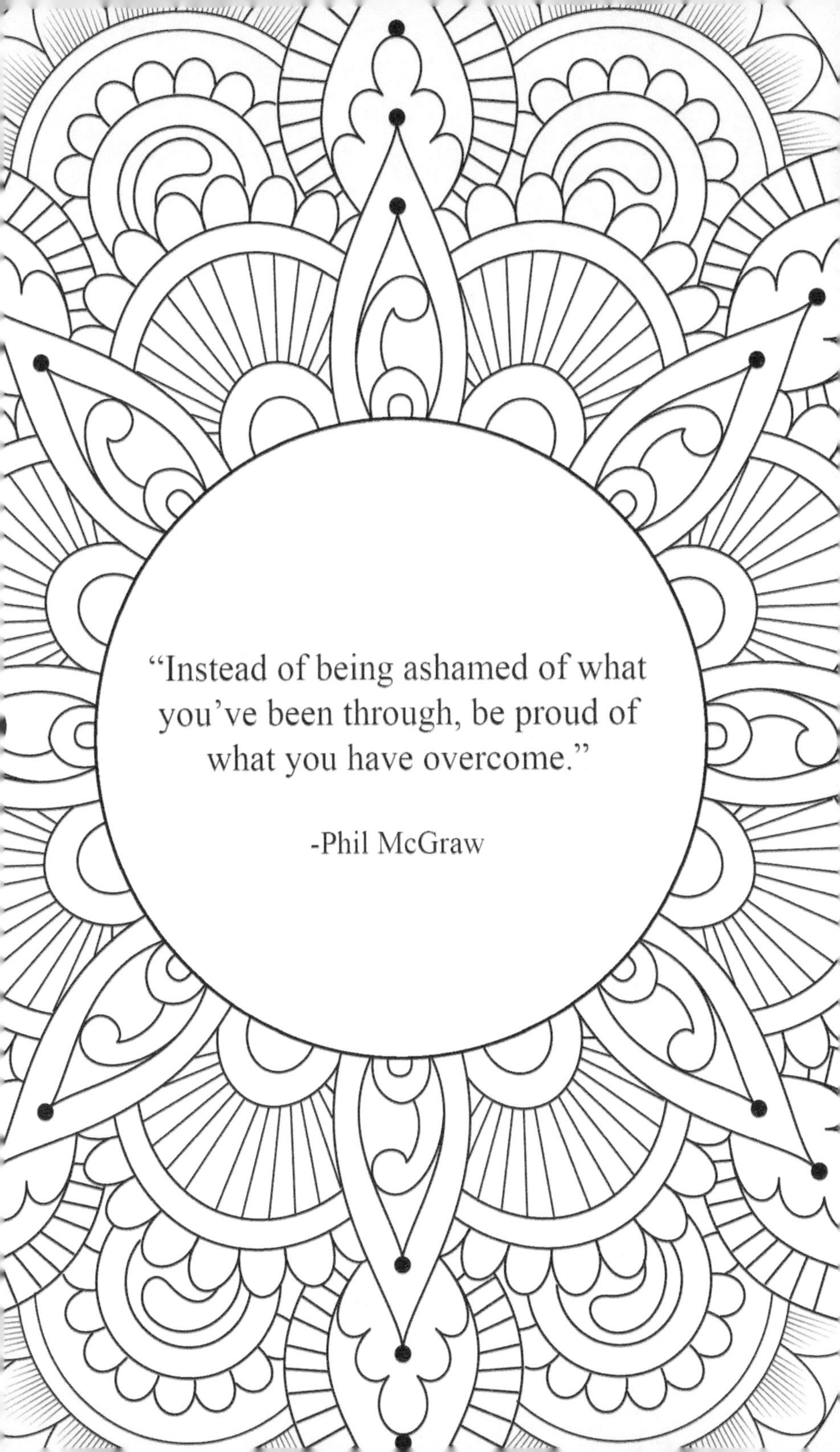
"Instead of being ashamed of what you've been through, be proud of what you have overcome."

-Phil McGraw

Chapter Thirteen

I CHOOSE GOOD ENERGY

AFTER THREE YEARS OF TRYING, I left our home and filed for divorce. Our marriage was irreconcilable. My husband blamed me for how he acted and I blamed him for honestly, *everything*. By this I was almost 27 years old and I was attempting to find my voice again (or maybe even for the first time). I needed to gain and regain my confidence.

Alone in my own space, I found myself thinking about my vulnerabilities a lot. Things like not loving myself and staying in a situation that made me question myself, and allowing someone to emotionally abuse me. Or accepting whatever was given instead of walking away from someone who refused to provide basics like affection, honesty, security and support.

Thinking that no one could possibly love me, and settling for a bad relationship because I thought it was as good as it could get for me. Not loving myself enough to believe I deserved more or take care of myself properly. Doubting I deserved anything more than the bare minimum and empty promises.

What I didn't consider was that these characteristics should have been guarded more carefully. I was traumatized, naive, and broken.

Then in stepped a charming, attractive man who seemed like the answer to my prayers.

Once again, in my mission to be accepted I found myself divulging my darkest secrets and greatest fears. But all that did was make me an easy target.

I learned the hard way that some people have agendas and they will not waver from their plan. They position themselves to learn your strengths and weaknesses to use them against you, leaving you to collect your broken pieces in an attempt to mend yourself for the umpteenth time. And although the narcissist inflicting the pain is to blame, it's important that we try to learn from these incidents because there are always red flags that we chose to ignore.

I've shared with you my stories. I wasn't someone with traditional abandonment issues, but I am someone with a tumultuous past. I have insecurities birthed from past trauma just like anyone else. But the root of these self-deprecating and self-sabotaging cycles was buried deep inside my subconscious. So, when I found someone that checked more than half my boxes and said those three little magic words, "I love you", I was desperate to please not knowing what lay ahead of me would be for a season instead of a lifetime.

And when we don't love ourselves, that happens more times than not. We question our strengths. We allow ourselves to be used and abused. When we accept whatever is given instead of walking away from someone that doesn't make us feel safe, confident, and heard we are doing ourselves the greatest disservice.

I settled because I thought "who else will want me." I doubted that I could be loved unconditionally. And on top of that, I allowed other people to tear me down and believed I was the problem. It was obvious I wasn't loving myself properly so I had to ask why. *Why don't you love yourself? How do you have love for everyone but yourself?*

It's important to reflect on the things you may have overlooked back then to sharpen your discernment. I say this because amongst those that are evil are good people who might mean well but don't know any better. And it's easy to put up walls that will leave those people on the outside too, so learning to listen to your gut is the best way to avoid this.

Anxiety is the feeling that there's danger present. When you feel anxious it is your body or mind telling you that there's a problem. Maybe that problem in your life needs to be solved, maybe it requires your immediate attention. But oftentimes it doesn't and if you're in tune with yourself you have a heightened sense of self-awareness that will allow you to take a step back and react appropriately. And if a situation warrants forgiveness you're more willing to give it because there's nothing nagging at you telling you that something is off.

CHOOSING GOOD ENERGY

Don't you think it would be wonderful to have a lifelong partner? A relationship where both partners thrive and are connected more profoundly without being clingy or dependent. The connection is a transformation from selfishness to selflessness, and you start to feel as if this relationship was everything you've been missing.

LAW OF ATTRACTION

Activating the law of attraction requires you to sincerely imagine what you want for yourself. If you want your dream career or a satisfying relationship, merely thinking about it is not sufficient. You must live and act on your dream. Because the law of attraction operates at a deeper level, crossing the conscious mind into subconscious depths. It is more than being positive; it means doing something to make your positive thoughts yield results.

Have you ever thought about why you attract a certain types of people, events, or situations? Why similar scenarios keep reoccurring in your life? It's an indication that you should reflect on your life and determine if there's a conflict between what you are doing and what you really want.

You may choose to ignore the inner voice calling to your insecurities and uncertainty but the more you ignore it, the stronger it becomes until it dominates your every waking thought and keeps you up at night.

The law states that if you are a fearful person, you attract other people who think that the world is unsafe. If you believe that you can't trust people around you, you attract events and situations that reaffirm those beliefs.

Your thoughts and actions emit a frequency of energy that's sent out into the universe. It is not dormant energy and creates results in line with your beliefs and thoughts. Which is why you should be mindful of what you think. It may mean that you will have to change your current concept of what your dream job or soulmate is. If you want to accomplish your life's dream, think of it, imagine it up, what it will look like, what it will *feel* like, and how you will enjoy it, and one day, your dreams will find you.

GUIDED MEDITATION TO ATTRACT POSITIVE ENERGY

You should sit in a comfortable position and close your eyes. Start taking slow deep breaths, in and out.

- Acknowledge the thoughts that have repeatedly come to mind lately, and remain alert to your reactions.
- Note if there are any limiting beliefs or toxic thoughts that might have prompted these negative thought patterns.
- Ask God, or your higher consciousness, to help you resolve your limiting beliefs in order to break the cycle of attracting more negative energy into your life.
- If there are multiple issues, pick the most harmful one. Go back in your mind to trace the source, all the way back to

when the issue first became present in your life? What was happening to you then? What type of environment were you in?

- Ask yourself how were you feeling then? Were you afraid, ashamed, or overwhelmed with guilt for making a mistake? How were your thoughts attracting negative circumstances one after another to reaffirm your negative beliefs?

- Gently allow yourself to come out of the negative space to heal your past wounds. Unless you let go of your past, history will repeat itself as you attract those emotions from your past into the present moment with a magnetic force of attraction.

- Remember, energy is neither created nor destroyed so imagine God's healing energy, or the energy of the universe, being drawn to you and releasing any feelings of blame or guilt. Feel that you are connected to the universe; accept the healing energy you are bringing in with gratitude.

- Bring your consciousness to the present moment and fill it with belief, faith, happiness and relief. Make your image strong, vivid, and unwavering.

- As you emerge from the mediation, give into your imagination and paint a more robust picture that will evoke positive emotions.

Exercise Fifteen: Loving Self Above All

When you're taking care of other people, it's often hard to take care of yourself. Even basic needs like feeding yourself can be a challenge.

In your companion journal, or on a separate sheet of paper, write down three ways you can take care of basic needs starting today. Then write down three ways you can treat yourself starting today. Treating yourself includes things you may have been conditioned to feel guilty about such as, a day off, splurging on yourself, or even alone time.

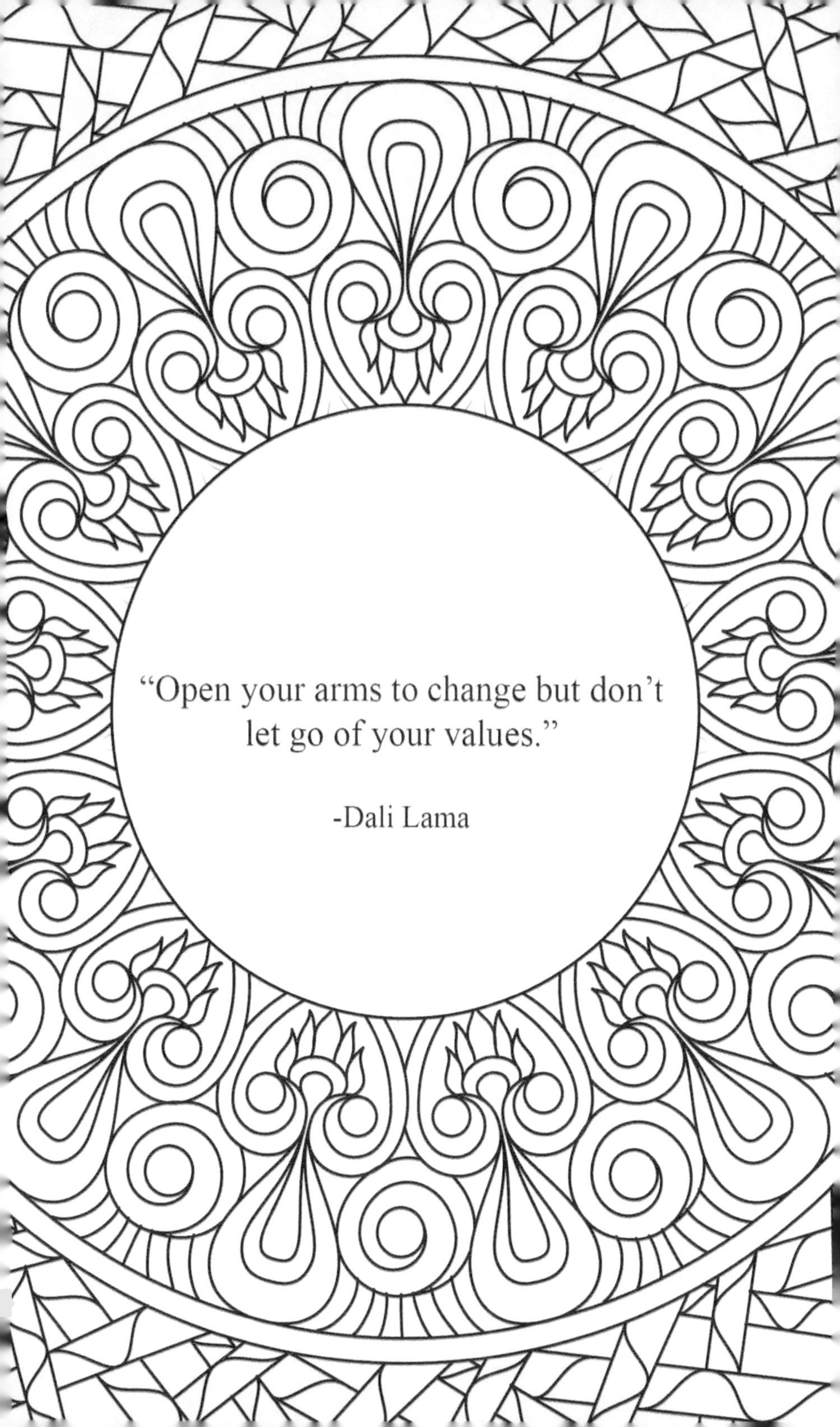
"Open your arms to change but don't
let go of your values."

-Dali Lama

Chapter Fourteen

THE FUTURE IS ALL HOPE

UNFORTUNATELY, uncovering how you genuinely feel is hard. We often lie to ourselves in an attempt to avoid feeling pain. Or, we tell ourselves we're not hurt by something because we feel as if talking about it won't change anything. I mentioned this briefly in the previous chapter, but I'd like to explore this topic a bit deeper because it's so very vital for our healing.

Let me start by telling you this: the road to self-healing starts with taking responsibility for your actions and your feelings. If you can do that, you are halfway there!

At the same time, you are only human. There will be times when you indeed feel too emotional. The human brain is wired to *react*, especially during times of great stress or crisis. Therefore being emotional in times of crisis is warranted, no matter what society may tell you.

You may have taught early in life to control your emotions or that it's unattractive to display "too much" emotion—especially negative emotion—in public. If you're anything like me, you're likely a master at masking your feelings to the point that you appear as though you're fine, even when you're not.

But, to go from mentally or emotionally unwell to living a long, happy and health life, it's essential to acknowledge the emotions our minds may have packed away like old clothes in the attics of our subconscious. Only when you've unpacked, examined, and even "tried them on" can you begin to let go of them and make way for what's to come.

Understandably, you may be afraid, not knowing what this type of emotional turmoil will bring or be like. So you try to control and minimize your hurt, compartmentalizing it instead. I can't stress enough that although it may seem easier, the reality is that your trauma will worsen. In spite of your sincere efforts to forget, distract yourself, or smother the pain, doing so would be like putting a Band-aid on an infected tattoo. Your tattoo won't heal until you drain the infection.

Here's another analogy: If I were to break a leg but refuse to see a doctor and have it properly set, the bone would indeed repair itself over time. However, the conditions would not be right. Therefore the chances of me regaining full functionality of my leg is unlikely. I'd probably always have a limp, or some other kind of issue.

Your emotions are just like that; until you create the conditions for healing, you will never function at 100%. Sometimes you need to get help to heal. You may think you don't need help, that you can do it all on your own. But recognize that this may be a defense mechanism you've established to avoid being let down or disappointed.

WHO ARE YOU?

My therapist once asked me if I thought I was beautiful. I responded by asking her if she wanted me to tell her what other people said about me or what I truly believed.

She told me to tell her what I thought about myself. "No, I don't think so," I responded.

This was right after she asked me to tell her ten nice things about myself. I answered by saying things like, "I'm smart, a good daughter, a good sister, and a good friend." It was obvious that at my core I didn't know my worth; I was still associating my value with how I supported other people.

It's never been easy for me to accept my God-given talents, or recognize my unique attributes. And I still struggle to see the things others do, all these years later.

The thing is, when you've been traumatized, it's common to struggle to see what all you bring to the table. Compliments will likely make you feel uncomfortable, or suspicious of someone's intentions. That is understandable.

But, there are happily-fulfilled people, then there are those who pretend to be happy, masking their emptiness and fear of rejection by withholding affection or safe-guarding their hearts. But which individuals are living a lie?

Is it truly possible to live a beautiful life where we can just be ourselves and be happy about it? Ten years ago—beaten down by my husband, my family, and the circumstances of my life—I would have said no, that no one can be happy inside *and* outside their homes. I would have told you that "the American dream" is just a fantasy and that happiness is short-lived. I would have insisted that it's impossible to have good health, financial security, a family unit, and happiness within yourself too.

But I've learned that that isn't true. Genuine happiness is not temporary. It is a state of mind. It is *joy*. Happiness cannot be possessed. It is a product of self-love and self-respect.

IMPORTANCE OF SELF-LOVE

Self-love supports your growth, your physical, emotional, and spiritual well-being and generates self-appreciation and self-love. In other words, self-love ensures that you value your own happiness. When you love yourself, you take care of your needs, and maintain healthy boundaries; you don't allow yourself to be at the beck and call of others. (Or at least, not until you've made sure your needs are attended to first.)

And because we are all different, expressions of self-love will be different for each of us. Let's explore what self-love might mean for you.

What is Your Self-Love Language?

- **Affirmations** - When you talk about yourself or even when you are talking *to* yourself, as we often do, your words are nice and caring. You acknowledge that everyone makes mistakes and accept that things may not have turned out the way you wanted because there's a better, more suitable, option for you.

- **Time** - You put yourself first. You prioritize your needs and wants, and spend time doing the things you enjoy, even if that means sometimes doing them by yourself.

- **Gifts** - You are confident in investing in yourself and your hobbies. You buy yourself gifts and spend money on things that bring you joy.

- **Service** - You set healthy boundaries that allow you time to rest and rejuvenate or do things that will make life easier. You maintain these boundaries, reexamining them as you see fit so you can continue to provide yourself with what you need when you need it.

- **Physical** - You do things that makes your body feel good and focus on your health. You forgive yourself when you have not been good to your body and avoid engaging in self-harming behavior.

Self-love is about self-preservation. You are showing others how you value yourself and how you expect to be treated while still taking care of your responsibilities or commitments. By practicing self-love, you are not dismissing or ignoring the needs of others.

What you are seeking from others is encouragement when you choose to make yourself a priority. Once they see how you value yourself others will start to value you as well. That starts with you appreciating your natural-born qualities and talents.

PRACTICING SELF-LOVE

Being aware of how to love yourself, and practicing loving yourself are two different things. Here's a few ways you can practice loving yourself that cost absolutely nothing.

Mindfulness

According to Kristen Neff, mindfulness allows you to accept an experience or set of circumstances with awareness but without judgment. It means overcoming hardships with patience and understanding, while self-love involves being kind to yourself at the same time.

When there's a stroke of bad luck and things don't go as we planned or hoped, many of us tend to obsess over what we should have, could have or would have done different. We hold ourselves fully responsible for what took place and hardly consider outside forces that contributed to things not working out, even if we know we put all our effort into it. This type of thinking isn't good. Instead, it adds to our feelings of guilt.

As Kristen Neff said, our self-criticism makes us both the offender and the offended.

Our first response to cruelty or transgressions is self-criticism, which causes us to suffer doubly from the consequences of the unfortunate incident that happened and our own self-punishment. It's important to hold ourselves accountable, yes. But as I said, living in the past, reevaluating details and scrutinizing what we could have done differently causes more harm than good.

Chronic self-criticism causes stress and damages our confidence, creating anxiety and depression.

Meanwhile, self-love and intentional self-compassion help us move on and let go. It helps us recognize that most things are not in our control, and makes us feel safe and secure. To practice it we must be mindful of our thoughts.

This type of approach to life helps you understand that there is a limit to what you can do and recognize when you have done enough.

Highly successful individuals who practice mindfulness know what they want in life, how much they should do to accomplish what they want, and when to call it a day.

PRACTICE HEALTHY HABITS

Healthy habits like balanced nutrition, adequate exercise and sleep, socializing, meditating, passions, and hobbies also all generate self-love.

Need-Based Actions

When practicing healthy habits and mindfulness you must base your actions on your *needs* rather than your *wants*. According to psychologists, our basic needs are few: food, water, and shelter for survival. As civilization advanced and humans progressed, "wants" later came into existence, although our *needs* remained straightforward: nourishment, safety, love, and self-esteem (*Lester et al., 1983*).

Our *wants*, on the other hand, are what often produce emotional turbulence. We get distracted and distraught by things we might want but consider unachievable, engaging in impulsive actions and getting into problematic situations, creating the perfect opportunity for us to grow frustrated with life.

Sometimes *wants* make us anxious. Therefore, we're far better off evaluating our needs.

Understanding Maslow's Theory of Self-Actualization

Abraham Maslow first introduced the idea of a hierarchy of needs in his research paper, "*A Theory of Human Motivation,*" published in 1943.

- First, we must try to fulfill our **basic physiological needs** like food and shelter.

- Our next priority is our **need for security and safety**. We look for jobs, maintain our health, and avert accidents.

- The third hierarchy is **social needs** like friendship, family, romantic relationship, community, etc.

- The fourth hierarchy of needs is complex. We **need to feel that we are valued and loved** by others, and to have some useful purpose for our lives.

- The next priority in the hierarchy is the **need for esteem, respect and recognition**.

- And the final hierarchy in Maslow's concepts of human needs is the **need for self-actualization**. It discusses how when we are more satisfied with ourselves, and more interested in personal growth, we are less worried about what others think of us. We look internally for self-approval and cultivate self-love and a sense of security, not relying on others for our source of happiness (*Cherry, 2022*).

Seeking Happiness

Self-love involves thriving and developing beyond a here today and gone tomorrow outlook on life. It allows us to find time to care for our well-being and happiness. It makes us feel secure in ourselves, we feel confident knowing that "I am and have always been there for myself." This feeling is fundamental to our happiness.

This type of happiness requires a sincere "flow" state of mind similar to self-actualization. Mihaly Csikszentmihalyi first described the "flow state" in his book "*Flow*." It is a state of deep concentration and total immersion in what you are doing without being concerned about time or other factors.

Focusing on your personal growth and development allows the flow of positive energy in your life. It recharges you when you feel depleted and gives you vitality and strength, wanting nothing more than to continue on this same path.

Have you ever seen a pianist play with complete absorption? The audience listens, mesmerized, and gives a standing ovation once the performance is over. But while playing the pianist had no idea how they'd enchanted the audience, too captivated by their own actions. This type of self-determination creates feelings of liberty, accomplishment, and long-lasting happiness.

TWELVE STEPS TO HAPPINESS

Even if you've struggled to develop a flow state of mind, be self-actualized or find true happiness, don't give up! Here are twelve steps that further break down how to reduce your levels of anxiety and depression, and enhance your mental and emotional well-being.

Do Not Compare Yourself with Others

Each one of us is distinct in thousands of ways. Your approach to any situation, no matter how common the circumstances might seem, will be unique. It is pointless to assume how someone else might react in a similar situation because we each come from different backgrounds, plus our pasts are different, so it is impossible to understand how an individual has accomplished what they have or why they're doing what they're doing.

Avoid Being Controlled by Others' Opinions

We can't create happiness for ourselves unless we allow ourselves time to relax and engage in the things we enjoy. You must avoid shouldering other people's responsibilities all the time. Which is why I have encouraged you to set boundaries and learn to say no even if it means disappointing others.

You can't make everyone happy, and each time you say yes to someone else, you say no to yourself. Therefore, the best thing you can do is be genuine and do more of what makes you happy.

Get Comfortable Making Mistakes

Everyone makes mistakes. Mistakes are learning experiences that help us to grow.

It may seem as if other individuals are perfect and never make mistakes, but this is far from the truth. Because there's no set path to follow and life involves countless interactions and other day-to-day variables, your mistakes are just another thing that makes you human. They also make you wiser and more compassionate.

Genuinely Care About Others

We are often judged by what we look like and how we dress—most of the time inaccurately—this is why we say to "never judge a book by its cover".

For the same reason, it's also important that you are mindful about how you interact with others. Smile a lot, have a positive mindset, and show a caring attitude by doing small things such as occasionally using their name when you're speaking. Actively listen to understand before responding, instead of just reacting or retaliating because you're triggered.

Show interest in what's being said, and give your full attention or communicate a later time when you're available to give the conversation the attention it deserves.

Avoid Toxic Relationships

A negative mindset attracts negativity. This kind of negative energy is depleting and harmful to anyone around it. Do not be afraid to get rid of toxic people and relationships.

I've been in toxic romantic relationships and friendships, and I know how much suffering it can cause. You can try your best to work around it but you'll inevitably be sucked into a whirlpool of emotional mayhem.

Face Your Fears

Your fears are legitimate. Denying they exist, won't make them go away. It is better to face your fears and analyze the reasons behind them. By being introspective you can uncover buried details and explore them logically to help you come to terms with most of your fears.

Trust In Yourself

Have faith that you are fully competent to make the right decisions for yourself. Above all, have faith in your ability and capacity to deal with any situation. Practice visualization techniques to inspire yourself or gain control.

This technique involves closing your eyes and imagining yourself doing the thing you wish to succeed at from start to finish. Complete the task in your mind step by step repeatedly to boost self-confidence.

For example, we all remember taking driving lessons.

I practiced much of my driving lessons at home, sitting on my bed, eyes closed, hands grabbing the imaginary wheel of my car while my feet played between the clutch and accelerator. I imagined myself maneuvering through traffic avoiding unmindful drivers and pedestrians, using hand-over-hand steering for navigating sharp turns, and stopping skillfully at various road signs and traffic signals.

By the time I got behind the wheel, I was so proficient that my ex thought I had driven a manual car before. My visualization of driving like a pro succeeded in calming my nerves and removing my self-doubts.

Find Happiness from Small Things in Life

We have all appreciated the perfect blue of a cloudless sky, a gorgeous sunset, or the beginning of quiet dawn. They don't take much to enjoy, and they come at no cost. On top of that, they remind us of the abundant beauty of nature and its magnificent creations.

You feel happy when your pet or child cheerfully welcomes you home, when you find money unexpectedly, or when your partner cooks a special dinner. These simple pleasures make life worthwhile and are things we should be grateful for.

Make Good Use of Opportunities

When opportunities knock at your door, be receptive and open to them. You sabotage yourself by waiting for the right time and the perfect situation that would allow you to begin pursuing your heart's desires.

But the right moment may be *right now*. And the ideal situation may not look like what you've imagined. So, utilize the opportunities that come your way, and let your destiny find you.

Experience Your Emotions Fully

Allow yourself to experience hardship and happiness fully. As a society, we have been encouraged to think of certain emotions like disappointment, grief, or anger as 'bad'. So when we are sad, we think it's bad that we feel that way.

We identify ourselves by our emotions, and this type of thinking makes us believe that we are the problem because we feel 'bad' emotions. Consequently, causing us to become an 'angry' or a 'depressed' person (*How to feel your feelings: Allowing yourself to feel fully*, 2021). Then, to avoid being labeled by these negative feelings we learn to suppress our emotions or just fake them. We are scared to express unfiltered sadness, afraid it will last indefinitely, or anger, fearing what people might think or say about us.

But it's important to know that when we avoid expressing our emotions fully, the energy of such emotions gets blocked inside our bodies. Unable to release itself, it persists, revealing itself explosively and, in fact, harmful behaviors like rage, self-mutilation or alcoholism.

An example of this is the situation where I was repeatedly sexually abused by a family member. Of course, a part of me despised him for what he'd done. Add to that the betrayal of my mother's inability or unwillingness to believe me, and her request to excuse his behavior "because he's family" broke my heart even more.

Wasn't I "family"? Wasn't I worth the same—if not greater—respect as her daughter? I was hurt on so many levels. So it was understandable how this buried pain haunted me later in life.

I couldn't come to terms with how it was affecting me until I acknowledged how I felt about it all. My emotions toward both my abuser and my mother made me feel like an angry, hateful person. But that feeling was simply a reaction to that traumatic event in my life.

I learned that to move on, and let go of my hurt and grief, I must initially admit how circumstances—like that abuse—truly made me feel then, and how I continued to feel even later on. Only then could I begin to work through those feelings and ultimately release them.

Be Bold

If you are a soft-spoken person, that's ok; but be courageous and speak your mind when necessary. Politeness is sometimes mistaken for cowardice. So, sit at the table—don't wait for permission— and join the conversation because your opinions are just as valuable as anyone else's (Stewart, 2018).

Be Nice to Yourself

"You must be fearless enough to give yourself the love you did not receive," said Oprah Winfrey. Loving ourselves is straightforward when things are going our way, but our self-confidence and self-esteem seem to abandon us when we feel rejected. When situations or events turn out differently than what we expected, we blame ourselves, judging our methods and actions.

We damage ourselves with self-criticism looking for comfort in others' arms, alcohol or drugs when we should be protecting and caring for ourselves the most.

This is where self-compassion plays the most significant role ever. Self-compassion, according to the pioneer of self-compassion Kristin Neff, has got three parts. They are self-kindness, feelings of common humanity, and mindfulness (Neff, 2010).

When opening yourself up to criticism, it's essential to filter through what actually applies to you and ignore your inner-critic's underlying fears and insecurities. Think of your best friend on their worst day, and speak to yourself as you would talk to them.

Practice this to allow room for error and growth. You must realize that you are worthy of the same things you want for your favorite person, and you deserve the same amount of consideration and empathy as anyone else.

Exercise Sixteen: Soaring Freely

In your companion journal, or on a separate sheet of paper, what healthy habits can you maintain each day to affect you positively? You can write one single habit for each day.

CONCLUSION

Like many of you, I, too, was not born privileged. I am a child of a broken home who lost parental guidance early in life. I made a poor choice regarding my partner, who I married. We had a son, and I believed everything would get better for me once I had a family. I was wrong.

I was caught up in an emotionally abusive relationship that promised no future for me. Every day I was diminished and tormented by my partner's indiscretions and ill manners toward me.

I tolerated insults and persevered, for the sake of my son and my love for my husband, till I could no more. My self-worth crumbled, impacting my mental health which took a toll on my body, until eventually it crashed. I went to therapy and was prescribed antidepressants along with proper counseling. After several difficult years I came across a therapist who finally guided me on the path of healing myself to self-actualization.

At last, I learned that we as humans find it hard to be happy because we remember hurtful moments from our past, forgetting the good ones that occurred in between the bad events. At best, our memories are like still photos, disjointed and out of context. We run them constantly through our minds to give them a movie-like reality.

But when we see the past better than it really was, the present worse than it actually is, and the future less resolved than it will ever be, we will remain in a state of brokenness never allowing ourselves to truly experience joy and happiness. Because remember, if nothing changes, nothing changes.

Now that you've discovered the path of self-actualization, continue the next step in the journey with me through my wellness organization Mindwell Body + Soul. Check out http://www.mindwellbodyand soul.com, or follow me on Instagram @tashiyannanoel to stay connected!

ACKNOWLEDGMENTS

I am humbled and blessed to have been shown so much love while creating this book over the last five years. When my mother gave me her blessing three years ago, it lit a fire within me that I assumed had been snuffed out long ago. It is because of her love and approval that I am able to share my story with you.

But before the writing began it was Dr. Ramona Hunt and her team of nurses, Bengy and Lucy, who comforted me during my darkest days. I am what most would call a difficult patient, but these women exhibited endearing kindness that was instrumental in changing my life.

The phenomenal therapist, Dr. Carol Watler, is always willing to say the things that are difficult for me to hear. The patience, guidance and understanding she's consistently provided during this journey has been invaluable to my growth.

Sincerest gratitude to Marvin Coleman, whose helpful suggestions and guidance helped improve the book in ways I couldn't have imagined.

I'm immensely grateful to Nandini, my researcher, and editor, Cynthia, who amplified my words with their depth and expertise. And to Reggie, who provided the books that created the foundation for this project.

Brittany, John, Tatiana, Jasmine, and Melaina—my kind, enthusiastic, and pushy support system that encouraged me to tell my personal story regardless of how others might feel. It is because of their boundless moral support that I was able to make it to the finish line.

Last, I will never be able to express how grateful I am to the rest of my family. Particularly my angel, Brenda Boyd, my father, my sister, my grandparents, Arthur and Lois, my aunt, Stephanie, and my uncle, Tyres. I hope I've made you all proud.

BIBLIOGRAPHY

Asad, F. (2020, September 24). How Romantic Movies Influence The Way In Which We Perceive Love? Psychologs.

Colino, S. (2022). Why Decluttering Is Important for Self-Care (and When It Isn't). Everyday Health.

De Waal, F., & Preston, S. D. (2017). Mammalian empathy: behavioural manifestations and neural basis. Nature reviews. Neuroscience, 18(8), 498–509. https://doi.org/10.1038/nrn.2017.72

Ferrari, J. R., Roster, C. A., Crum, K. P., & Pardo, M. A. (2018). Procrastinators and Clutter: An Ecological View of Living with Excessive "Stuff." Current Psychology, 37(2), 441–444. https://doi.org/10.1007/s12144-017-9682-9

Griffen, T. C., Naumann, E., & Hildebrandt, T. (2018). Mirror exposure therapy for body image disturbances and eating disorders: A review. Clinical Psychology Review, 65, 163–174. https://doi.org/10.1016/j.cpr.2018.08.006

How Much Sleep Do I Need? (n.d.). Https://Www.Cdc.Gov/Sleep/About_sleep/How_much_sleep.Html.

How To Feel Your Feelings: Allowing Yourself To Feel Fully. (2021, February 25). Https://Www.Livingbetterlivesnwa.Com/Blog/2021/2/24/How-to-Feel-Your-Feelings-Allowing-Yourself-to-Feel-Fully.

Jennison, C. (2020, December 11). Emotional Health vs. Mental Health: The Real Difference. Https://Eddinscounseling.Com/Emotional-Health-vs-Mental-Health/.

Lebow, H. (2021, June 10). How Childhood Trauma May Affect Adult Relationships. Psychcentral.

Martin, A. J., & Marsh, H. W. (2008). Academic buoyancy: Towards an understanding of students' everyday academic resilience. Journal of School Psychology, 46(1), 53–83. https://doi.org/10.1016/j.jsp.2007.01.002

Maslow, A.H. (1943) A Theory of Human Motivation. Psychological Review, 50, 370-396. http://dx.doi.org/10.1037/h0054346

Neff, K. D., & Dahm, K. A. (2015). Self-Compassion: What It Is, What It Does, and How It Relates to Mindfulness. In Handbook of Mindfulness and Self-Regulation (pp. 121–137). Springer New York. https://doi.org/10.1007/978-1-4939-2263-5_10

Nesse, R. M., & Stein, D. J. (2019). How evolutionary psychiatry can advance psychopharmacology. Dialogues in clinical neuroscience, 21(2), 167–175. https://doi.org/10.31887/DCNS.2019.21.2/rnesse

Rettew, D. C., Vink, J. M., Willemsen, G., Doyle, A., Hudziak, J. J., & Boomsma, D. I. (2006). The genetic architecture of neuroticism in 3301 Dutch adolescent twins as a function of age and sex: a study from the Dutch twin register. Twin research and human genetics : the official journal of the International Society for Twin Studies, 9(1), 24–29. https://doi.org/10.1375/183242706776403028

Roster, C. A., Ferrari, J. R., & Peter Jurkat, M. (2016). The dark side of home: Assessing possession 'clutter' on subjective well-being. Journal of Environmental Psychology, 46, 32–41. https://doi.org/10.1016/j.jenvp.2016.03.003

Saxbe, D. E., & Repetti, R. (2010). No Place Like Home: Home Tours Correlate With Daily Patterns of Mood and Cortisol. Personality and Social Psychology Bulletin, 36(1), 71–81. https://doi.org/10.1177/0146167209352864

Stewart-Brown S. (1998). Emotional wellbeing and its relation to health. Physical disease may well result from emotional distress. BMJ (Clinical research ed.), 317(7173), 1608–1609. https://doi.org/10.1136/bmj.317.7173.1608

Swanson, H. L., & Ferrari, J. R. (2022). Older Adults and Clutter: Age Differences in Clutter Impact, Psychological Home, and Subjective Well-Being. Behavioral Sciences, 12(5), 132. https://doi.org/10.3390/bs12050132

Wilson, D. S., & Wilson, E. O. (2007). Rethinking the theoretical foundation of sociobiology. The Quarterly review of biology, 82(4), 327–348. https://doi.org/10.1086/522809

www.ingramcontent.com/pod-product-compliance
Lightning Source LLC
Chambersburg PA
CBHW021448150726
47989CB00001B/447